MAL WALDEN'S
AUSSIE
MYTHS
MYSTERIES
AND MEMORIES

Published by Brolga Publishing Pty Ltd
ABN 46 063 962 443
PO Box 452
Torquay Victoria 3228
Australia

email: markzocchi@brolgapublishing.com.au

All rights reserved. No part of this publication may be reproduced, stored in a retrieval system or transmitted in any form or by any means electronic, mechanical, photocopying, recording or otherwise without prior permission from the publisher.

Copyright © 2022 Mal Walden

National Library of Australia
Cataloguing-in-Publication data
    Mal Walden, author.
       ISBN 9781920785185 (paperback)

 A catalogue record for this book is available from the National Library of Australia

Printed in Australia
Cover design by Luke Harris, Working Type Studio
Typesetting by Scott Riddle

BE PUBLISHED

Publish through a successful publisher
National Distribution to Australia & New Zealand
International Distribution to the United Kingdom
Ebooks Worldwide
Sales Representation to South East Asia

Email: markzocchi@brolgapublishing.com.au

Table of Contents

Beasts from Billabongs and Beyond — 1

UFOs — Myth, Mystery or Malarkey? — 15

Bass Strait — Australia's Bermuda Triangle? — 35

Mahogany and Missing Maritime — 41

Lost, Missing or Murdered? — 51

Subterranean Secrets — 73

Tunnels to Nowhere? — 85

Mystery of Buried Bullions — 89

Supernatural Resurgence — 101

Myths or Legends — 111

Beasts from Billabongs and Beyond

State Library Victoria, National Library of Australia

It is said that searching for signs of mythical beasts is akin to following the trail of droppings from the beasts themselves. There is the distinct whiff of fallacy in their wake, infused with a little ambiguity and a heavy dose of Aussie humour. Yet news reports continue to surface from time to time, giving life-supporting sustenance to our most elusive beasts.

The Bunyip

1818: One of the first accounts of a Bunyip refers to the discovery of the remains of a large unknown freshwater animal by early explorer Hamilton Hume at Lake Bathurst in New South Wales. The animal was not called a Bunyip but described 'as much like a hippopotamus or manatee'.

1835: Fossilised bones were discovered in the Wellington Caves, New South Wales. British anatomist Sir Richard Owen described the bones as the remains of prehistoric marsupial Diprotodon.

1845: The *Geelong Advertiser* announced the discovery of fossils found near Geelong under the headline 'Wonderful Discovery of a new Animal'.

1846: A skull was found in the Murrumbidgee River near Balranald and placed in the Australian Museum in Sydney. It was labelled as a Bunyip but later proven to be the skull of a disfigured calf.

Fusing those post-colonial reports with Aboriginal cultural stories is perhaps where the Bunyip was born into Australian folklore. However, the search to confirm its existence is about as murky as the muddied waters of their mythical habitat.

The word itself, translated by indigenous Australians, comes from 'devil' or 'evil spirit'. According to Rex Gilroy, author of *Mysterious Australia*, a large mythical creature from Aboriginal Dreaming stories was long said to "lurk in swamps, billabongs, creeks and waterholes". From that point on, the image of the Bunyip becomes a little more obscure and dependent on the eye of the beholders.

"It is of immense size, possesses deadly claws, powerful hind legs and a brightly coloured chest. It has a head resembling an emu, with a long bill, at the extremity of which is a transverse projection on each side, with serrated edges like the bone of the stingray. Its body and legs partake of the nature of the alligator. The hind legs are remarkably thick and strong, and the fore legs are much longer, but still of great strength. When in the water it swims like a frog, and when on shore it walks on its hind legs with its head erect, in which position it measures twelve or thirteen feet in height." *Geelong Advertiser*, July 2, 1845.

It has also been noted that the characteristics were similar to the then undiscovered Australian cassowary.

Meanwhile other descriptions recorded in the newspapers at the time and by the Royal Australian Historical Society have varied depending on the area it supposedly existed.

"It looked like an enormous starfish," while some claimed "it resembled the head of a snake with a beard".

Others argued "it had a dog-like face, on a crocodile-like head, with dark fur, a horse-like tail, flippers, walrus-like tusks, and a duck-like bill".

Then there is the 'seal-dog variety' most often described as being between one to two metres long with a shaggy black or brown coat. According to early post colonisation reports, these Bunyips had "round heads resembling a bulldog, prominent ears, no tail, and whiskers like a seal or otter. The long-necked variety had large ears, small tusks with a head like a horse".

The Bunyip has long been described by First Nations peoples as amphibious, nocturnal and inhabiting lakes, rivers and swamps. Stories passed down describe them as swimming swiftly with fins or flippers, having a loud, roaring call and feeding on crayfish. Historians have also noted that seals and sea lions often ventured far up the estuaries and river systems.

Some legends portrayed Bunyips as bloodthirsty predators of humans, particularly women and children. This supports a Dreaming songline that the water spirit called 'Mulyawonk' was deliberately created by Aboriginal elders as a warning to rivals poaching their fish and to their children who risked venturing too close to dangerous waters.

Perhaps the latter theory has some merit. As a boy scout in the mid 1950s attached to the 1st Frankston unit, my first overnight bivouac took place on the banks of the Bunyip River, south east of Melbourne. The traditional initiation for first time scouts always included searches for 'hip-holes', 'long-waits' and 'sky-hooks'. With each assignment I will always remember the troop leaders warning not to venture too close to the riverbank for 'fear of the Bunyip'.

In hindsight it was not unlike the traditional Bunyip warning to First Nation children created by elders and simply passed down through the ages. Whatever its origins, through word of mouth the Bunyip's reputation has been kept alive to become part of Australian folklore — not unlike another beast from beyond our billabongs: the Yowie.

Sources: National Library, *Out of the Shadows: Mysterious Animals of Australia*, by Robert Holden, Tony Healy and Paul Cropper.

The Yowie

European colonists first began reporting 'foul-smelling' ape-like creatures in Australia shortly after colonisation. The first sighting was said to have taken place near Sydney Cove, New South Wales in 1795. By the 1880s further accounts of 'Australian Apes' began to appear in published media, as did the name, 'Yowie'.

1842: "The natives of Australia...believe in...[the] YAHOO...This being they describe as resembling a man...

of nearly the same height, ...with long hair hanging down from the head over their features... the arms extraordinarily long, furnished at the extremities with great talons. Altogether, they describe it as a hideous monster of an unearthly character and ape-like appearance."

Other reported sightings took place on the rugged Carrai Plateau west of Kempsey, New South Wales in 1842, the Snowy Mountains in 1860 and the Jamieson Valley, Victoria in 1875.

Descriptions in the print media of the time of the Yowie were always consistent to that of "a hairy and ape-like creature standing upright at between 2.1 and 3.6 metres tall".

The Yowie's feet were described as much larger than human feet but more varied than the feet of America's 'Bigfoot'. The Yowie's nose was described as wide and flat. While some described the creature as timid and shy, others warned the Yowie could become violent or aggressive.

During the years of colonisation, Australian Aboriginal people often warned British colonists to beware of huge ape-like creatures that lurked in the rugged mountains and deep forests, telling stories that they exist in their Dreaming. They knew them by many names but after colonists began to report hair-raising encounters with the hulking, foul-smelling creatures, they were being referred to as simply 'Australian apes', 'Youries'…or even 'Yahoos'.

Another story from Aboriginal sources suggests that at one time these creatures lived in tribes and were the original inhabitants of the country.

In 1882, amateur naturalist Henry James McCooey reported having seen an 'indigenous ape' on the south coast of New South Wales, between Batemans Bay and Ulladulla.

"I should think that if it were standing perfectly upright it would be nearly five feet (1.5m) high. It was tailless and covered with very long black hair, which was of a dirty red or snuff-colour about the throat and breast. Its eyes, which were small and restless, were partly hidden by matted hair that covered its head...I threw a stone at the animal, whereupon it immediately rushed off".

While the origin of the Yowie appears steeped in Aboriginal historical stories, their reputation has since become a modern zoological mystery. Unlike the Bunyip from our billabongs, Yowie reports extend far and wide across the continent — from the Australian outback to coastal regions and likened to Americas 'Bigfoot' or the 'Yeti' (the abominable snowman from the Himalayas).

In 2010, a Canberra man reported that he had disturbed an animal in his garage which he described as "a juvenile, covered in hair, with long arms that almost touched the ground".

Today, they are all generally referred to as Yowies and the list of modern-day eyewitnesses have included zoologists, rangers, surveyors and possibly even members of the elite Special Air Service Regiment, although I couldn't confirm this. While reports continue from time to time, more so during the wet tropical season in northern Australia, no specific scientific evidence of their existence has ever emerged. The Yowie appears to be almost as elusive as the mystery of the Drop Bear.

Sources: *The Yowie: In Search of Australia's Bigfoot*, Healey and Cropper. State Library Victoria.

The Drop Bear

In researching Australian mythology one clear observation emerges. If we truly believe in something, it not only becomes a profound influence on our lives but can also exert a powerful influence on others, whatever form that belief should take or however elusive or absurd it may appear.

When such beliefs are continually circulated, there is the frightening possibility that what began as an absurd myth can morph into urban legend, or even take on a new life of its own.

Take for example the case of the Australian Drop Bear, described as a "fiendish, carnivorous, blood-sucking koala-like animal that launch themselves from trees on unsuspecting victims below".

Archaeological evidence points to a prehistoric marsupial lion, named *Thylacoleo carnifex,* which lived and hunted in Australia thousands of years ago, and possibly had the ability to climb and leap from trees. Some have suggested this is the true origin of the Drop Bear myth.

Recent developments in Australian archaeology have fuelled media speculation regarding the possible origins of this legend describing an assemblage of scratch marks found at Tight Entrance Cave in West Australia. The cave is a known site for the prehistoric marsupial lion. *National Geographic* suggests this species called the *Thylacoleo* "prowled Australia during the last Ice Age". Then there is the mammoth bear (now extinct) said to have grown to approximately five metres. Some sources also describe a nocturnal variety (*Thylarctos plummetus vampirus*) that drank the blood of its prey.

According to the story, the common Drop Bear ranges in size from roughly that of a leopard (30 kg) to a large dog (45 kg), hence the similarity in size to the lion. Today, Australians have taken the Drop Bear to an entirely new level. The Museum of Australia has even created a fake information page on its website.

According to their records: "The Drop Bear legend tells of a large, arboreal, predatory marsupial related to the Koala that 'drops' on its prey. Drop Bears supposedly hunt by ambushing ground dwelling animals from above, waiting up to as much as four hours to make a surprise kill. Once prey is within view, the Drop Bear will drop as much as eight metres to pounce on top of the unsuspecting victim. The initial impact often stuns the prey, allowing it to be bitten on the neck and quickly subdued."

Their satirical 'educational' webpage depicts the Drop Bear as having several defining traits including a substantial physical stature and broad, powerful premolars rather than canines, indicative of a carnivorous diet.

Researchers from James Cook University have also explored "the Australian Drop Bear urban legend" likening it to folktales of other countries and their mysteries of mythological creatures — think 'Yetis' the 'Loch Ness Monster' and the American 'Jackalope' (described as a jackrabbit with antelope horns) and of course 'Bigfoot'. But with the Drop Bear, there's a twist. No Australian actually believe it exists — it's just used to scare people, typically foreign tourists.

Travel website *Tripadvisor* has even been forced to respond to messages from concerned travellers, particularly Americans.

Tourist: Hi there, I am really worried about drop bears! I am due to arrive in Australia and I have done my research on spiders and jellyfish but how do I avoid drop bears? (2006)

Tripadvisor: Don't travel on April 1 and you will be fine. There is a spray-on product called 'Bear'O'Guard'...just be aware that it isn't 100% effective on weekdays.

The legend of the Drop Bear would appear to have been created for the media during its non-rating period, or what we call 'the silly season'. It's just that the season never seems to end.

Puma/Panther?

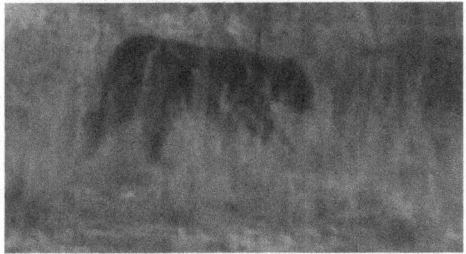

Mystery sighting

One of my first assignments as a junior reporter with the Seven Network concerned the perennial saga of a mystery animal roaming parts of Victoria. Depending on the area it was last seen it kept adopting new identities 'The Moe Monster', 'The Macclesfield Marauder' or 'The Trentham Tiger'.

On a cold damp morning in August 1973, after tramping across a soggy paddock in the outer area of Pakenham, east of Melbourne, I was about to bestow yet another title on this elusive beast. In true tabloid tradition I called it the 'Pakenham Panther' and to this day panther or puma seems to have become the popular people's choice.

With sheep dogs snapping at each other and a farmer in no better mood, we were led to a tree at the far end of his paddock. Lodged in a limb high above us were the distinct remains of a half-eaten sheep. The farmer was adamant it wasn't the victim of a wedge-tailed eagle.

"It's the bloody panther," he said. "It's back."

The legend of big black cats has been one of Australia's most enduring mysteries, with hundreds of sightings in Victoria since the 1880s. They have been recorded from as far as Gippsland in the east, the Otways to the south, the Grampians in the west, the high country to the north and as far as New South Wales and South Australia.

Reports have described the animals as being sleek, black and with a long-coiled tail resembling the feline features of a leopard or puma. There are a number of theories as to what the big cats are and even where they originated. These include: they are a surviving relative of *Thylacoleo carnifex*, which was once Australia's largest marsupial carnivore; pumas brought to Australia by American gold miners in the 19th century; descendants of US Army mascots from World War 2 which were released into the wild after the war when troops departed; big cats that escaped from travelling carnivals, circuses or private zoos; overgrown, feral black cats. The historical material is all based on anecdotal reportage that has contributed to the mystification of the subject, or blurred and distant photos.

In August 1973, I stood looking up at the half-eaten carcass of this dead sheep remembering earlier that year reporting from a similar scene at Bacchus Marsh where a farmer and his family reported "a six-foot black furred monster cat dragging a dead calf across their paddock".

Two years later I found myself reporting on Hastings farmer Todd Anderson, who lost three pigs and two calves in a space of a week. Each night they were literally carried off by an animal that left enormous claw and pad marks in the soil.

Reports of cat-like monsters have emerged over generations and continue to this day, but without any credible footage to back up the claims. As with my first report we took plaster casts of the pads and claw markings to the Melbourne Zoo who confirmed only that they were feline.

In 2012 a State Government report into Victoria's big cats claimed the existence of panthers and big cats was "highly unlikely", but reserved a conclusion that "evidence would be found". However, a study by Deakin University concluded the existence of big cats in the Grampians was "demonstrated beyond reasonable doubt".

One of the most recently reported sightings took place on the Mornington Peninsula, south of Melbourne. In June 2021, Michael Corr, 36, was walking through the Tootgarook wetlands with his 11-year-old son when they encountered a huge cat-like creature. Since going public he has received dozens of calls from other locals confirming they too had seen a panther in their area.

Several weeks earlier near Mount Beauty in Victoria's high country, Amanda Dutton reported a huge black panther while driving home from football with her children. "It would have been as high as our kitchen bench," she told her friends. "It was less than 20 metres away from us and its tail was at least a metre long." Instead of being ridiculed when she told her friends, they all laughed. "It's the Mitta Panther," they said. They had all seen it.

Pumas, panthers, leopards, cougars or simply huge feral cats? It's a perennial story that stirs the imagination, like the mystery of our striped tiger.

Sources: State Library Victoria, extracts from *Good News* (Brolga Publication).

Tasmanian Tiger

Well before colonisation, the thylacine could be found roaming across the entire continent of Australia, even as far as southern New Guinea. However, around 2,000

years ago, they became confined to the small island state of Tasmania, which is why they became known as the Tasmanian tiger.

When Europeans first settled in Tasmania the animal was rarely seen, however by 1830, after continuing attacks on sheep, bounty schemes began to be established offering money in exchange for dead thylacines.

By the 1920s, sightings of the Tasmanian tiger in the wild had become extremely rare until 1930, when a farmer from Mawbanna named Wilf Batty, shot and killed the last known wild specimen.

The only living Tasmanian tiger, which had been captured in the Florentine Valley in 1933, was then transferred to the Hobart Zoo where it lived until September 7, 1936. Thus the final thylacine, which became known as 'Benjamin', died in captivity.

Are Tasmanian tigers still alive?

Since Benjamin's death in 1936 there have been many unconfirmed encounters of Tasmanian tigers and many in recent times.

• In 2005, two German tourists, Klaus Emmerichs and Birgit Jansen, claimed to have snapped two pictures of a live Tasmanian tiger near Derwent Bridge in the rugged Central Highlands.

• In 2017, three investigators including Adrian Richardson, who had been hunting the thylacine for 26 years, captured video of what they claimed was a Tasmanian tiger near Hobart. "I don't *think* it's a thylacine...I *know* it's a thylacine," Richardson said.

• In 2018, a Sydney man revealed home video of a creature he believed to be a Tasmanian tiger.

• On January 4, 2019, Victorian farmer, Peter Groves, attracted media interest after allegedly spotting a thylacine while walking near Clifton Springs in Victoria. Groves managed to pull out his mobile phone and snap a picture of the creature which he then uploaded to social media. He described the specimen as "funny looking…with a big, long tail and stumpy ears".

All reports have failed to convince the experts, including one of the latest when in 2021 veteran thylacine hunter Neil Waters announced to the media he had irrefutable proof the Tasmanian tiger was not extinct. Despite his video and photographic evidence, he also failed to convince the experts. Several years ago, during a media luncheon with former colleagues the subject of stories we all wished we had covered in our careers was discussed. Among our group was one of Australia's foremost respected newspaper photographers. On the condition of maintaining his anonymity, he recounted his encounter with a thylacine. He claimed he was returning from an assignment in Gippsland, Victoria when the animal stepped out of bushes and stood in the glare of his car's headlights. "I got out and it remained quite still. We both just looked at each other before it loped back into the bush."

We all asked the same question. Why didn't you grab your camera and capture it as proof? The reasons he gave were twofold. Had his photo failed to convince the sceptics his reputation would have suffered irreparably. But the main reason he gave was a fear that once it was in the public domain the area would have been invaded by fortune seekers and bounty hunters. "I know it exists," he said, "and that's all that matters. Case closed." But is it?

All urban legend is folklore, though not all folklore is urban legend - Mikel J. Koven.

UFOs
Myth, Mystery or Malarkey?

Photograph of the supposed 1966 Westall UFO encounter - UIG.

In an age where technology has revolutionised the camera, UFO media reports invariably feature distant, blurred or mock-up images. We are still waiting for that crystal clear close-up of a 'flying saucer' and definitive proof of their existence. Extraordinary claims always require extraordinary evidence and I can tell you it has not been for want of trying.

UFOs?

Long before mainstream media coined the term UFO (Unidentified Flying Object) Australia had already documented what was believed to have been our first extra-terrestrial encounter in 1863.

Still regarded as one of the strangest sightings of unknown flying craft, Paramatta surveyor Fred Birmingham wrote of his experience in a 15-page document titled *A Machine to go through the air*. Birmingham's description of "strange dreams, floating heads, spirit voices and a flying ark" has since been deemed a genuine document made by a reliable witness. For the following 80 years sightings became far more frequent before peaking during the years of the Cold War.

In 1947, an American businessman, Kenneth Arnold, claimed he had seen a formation of nine high-speed objects while flying his small plane near Washington. From a subsequent newspaper report describing them as "like saucers skipping on water" the term 'flying saucer' was born.

That same year an American rancher came across mysterious wreckage near an army airfield in Roswell, New Mexico. Local papers reported it was the remains of a flying saucer and while the US military dismissed it as just a weather balloon, many eyewitnesses and leaked photographs suggested otherwise. Those denials simply fanned the flames of a conspiracy and cover-up, just as UFO researchers today accuse authorities of doing exactly the same in Australia.

Westall, 1966

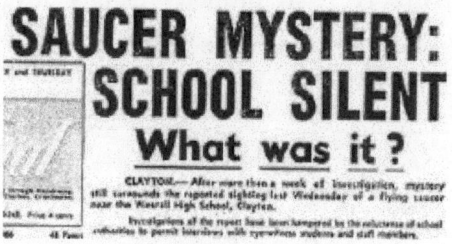

- The year began with news of the resignation of Australia's longest serving Prime Minister Sir Robert Menzies.
- Three young Beaumont children were abducted during a trip to Glenelg Beach, Adelaide.
- On February 14 we all faced the confusing conversion to decimal currency.

As these stories began shaping my fifth year in media, so too was the groundswell of opposition building against the Vietnam war. In early April we were preparing for more protests over the controversial flight of Australia's first conscripts bound for the war zone. But then no one could have foreseen another flight would capture the headlines, leading to conspiracy theories and cover-ups that would continue long after the Vietnam war was lost.

On Wednesday April 6, 1966 a lunchtime school bell rang out at Westall High (now Westall Secondary College) in the Melbourne suburb of Clayton. As the students began to pour out of their classrooms and onto the oval for their lunch break, a cry suddenly echoed across the grounds, "Flying saucers…flying saucers".

At least three unidentified objects were seen circling the Westall High School and the nearby primary school. Several high school students ran back to alert their Year Nine science teacher Andrew Greenwood. "I looked up and saw one object in the sky directly over the far side of the oval. It was a classic cigar shaped object…it looked like grey metal." Greenwood would continue to recount that moment in his life for the next 50 years. "That's what it looked like, a grey, cylindrical, cigar-shaped object which moved with precision in the sky."

As the students and teachers stood transfixed to the objects in the sky one appeared to peel off before landing behind a group of pine trees on adjoining land to the school known as The Grange.

Minutes after it landed a number of students climbed the fence for a closer look including student Terry Peck. "I didn't see it land but I saw it on the ground in front of me. I could feel heat and a sort of buzzing sound. I could see purple lights all around it". Several students later admitted they had been close enough to touch it. It was then the object suddenly rose off the ground and kept rising to probably three or four meters before joining the other two in the sky above. According to Greenwood, "it tilted to one side as it rose into the sky".

The entire episode was witnessed by more than 200 students, teachers and nearby residents. Some indicated the objects were also being monitored by several light planes which had arrived from the nearby Moorabbin airport. Greenwood would later describe the planes as doing everything possible to approach the objects. "How they all avoided collision I will never know. It was the most amazing flying I had ever seen. Every time they got too close to one object it would gradually accelerate, move away from them and then stop." Greenwood described the action as a 'cat and mouse game' which continued for about 20 minutes before the UFO that had landed then sped away and vanished. As did the others.

While all 200 students and staff were watching in fascination, the headmaster was calling the local airport seeking an explanation to the extraordinary events. The authorities had now been alerted and so began a concerted effort to shut it down. Year 8 student Suzanne Savage would later tell the *Saturday Age* that principal Frank Samblebe immediately called an urgent assembly and ordered them not to speak to anyone about what they had seen. "He said he didn't want to hear anymore about this nonsense and we were not to discuss it ever again."

However, attempts to completely silence the incident had failed. Among the first to question the witnesses was a reporter from the *Dandenong Journal*. Pressed further to describe the object Greenwood would later attempt to downplay a question of UFOs. "I'm not going to say it was a 'flying saucer', that's too emotive language…but it was though, of the shape you would see if you had a saucer slightly tipped on its side." He went on to describe the object as "a silvery disc with a purple hue, roughly the size of about two cars".

Others too had already spoken out and while some descriptions may have varied slightly the one consistency was its shape and speed of flight. Within 30 to 40 minutes air force and army personnel were said to have arrived in trucks before immediately stationing guards at different points, stopping anyone from going into the landing area at The Grange. They allegedly warned witnesses never to tell anyone what they believed they had seen. It was, they said, "an errant high-altitude weather balloon".

Fourteen days later Greenwood said he was paid a visit at his home by two men on official government business. "One was in plain clothes, the other wore an air force uniform. They told me I was wrong and hadn't seen anything." When he tried to explain to them that he had been there and they hadn't, he said they became threatening. "I was told that I should not go public as I was clearly drunk at the time while on duty at the school. Should I say anything I would be reported to the education department and told I would lose my job." Several students and teachers reported similar threats by officials who made no secret of their attempts to shut the incident down.

Fifty-five years later Greenwood remained just as defiant, remembering the official pressure being applied. However, some time later he said he had been approached by an American official investigating the Westall UFO sighting. Professor James McDonald identified himself as having formally represented the US Navy but was then assigned to an American government agency specifically investigating UFOs. McDonald revealed he had already received 50 to 60 reports of UFO incidents since his arrival in Australia and New Zealand. He was investigating if these reports tallied with similar sightings in the USA and whether they posed a global phenomenon or security risk.

But unlike his other investigations the Westall incident was unique. Never had a UFO sighting been reported by so many reliable witnesses at the same time. Descriptions he said were consistent in that the object had been seen to hover, then accelerate in controlled conditions before travelling a considerable distance to another part of the sky within seconds. On the 40th anniversary of Westall, eyewitnesses stood by their initial statements, maintaining that they had been visited by a UFO and accused the military of attempting a cover-up. There have since been suggestions that the incident resulted from a government program called 'Project HIBAL' established in the 1960s to sample radiation from the controversial Maralinga nuclear tests using a high-altitude balloon. But witnesses dispute this, citing the controlled speed at which it flew.

On Sunday May 30, 2021 the Seven Network revisited Westall 55 years after the incident. According to respected five-time Walkley award winning journalist Ross Coulthart, the Australian government had once held thousands of UFO reports going back decades, "all stamped secret or top secret including hovering craft, flying saucers and black triangles". But he said, "there is one very secret report which wasn't in the archives yet is regarded as Australia's greatest UFO mystery of all time".

Many attempts had been made by Australian media groups seeking requests through Freedom of Information (FOI) for files pertaining to UFO sightings across the country. According to the *Sydney Morning Herald*, Government officials also came back empty-handed claiming the file had gone missing and was officially 'deemed lost.' Australian military sources say they stopped taking reports of UFOs in late 2000, instead directing any sightings to the police.

While the denials have only contributed to the mystery of UFOs there is another theory feeding the appetite of conspiratorialists. Did the same UFO return 12 years later?

Sources: *Sydney Morning Herald*, Newscorp, *Dandenong Journal*, HSV7, State Library of Victoria.

Frederick Valentich

Valentich with his Cessna

Very few cases have captured the imagination or stirred the debate over mystery UFOs more than the disappearance of Frederick Valentich in 1978. Whatever happened to Valentich, who disappeared while flying a single engine Cessna over Bass Strait on October 21 that year, may never be known. What we do know are his last words to air traffic control: "That strange aircraft is hovering on top of me again. It is hovering, and it's not an aircraft… It is…" A sound was heard before that final transmission ended. So began one of the most dramatic aviation mysteries since the disappearance of Amelia Earhart on July 3, 1937.

The sun was setting around 7:00pm, when Valentich took off from Moorabbin Airport piloting a rented single engine Cessna. He took a south easterly course towards King Island in Bass Strait. Four minutes later (7:06pm) he radioed Melbourne Air Flight Service at Tullamarine and spoke to controller Steve Robey.

Valentich: Is there any known traffic below five thousand feet?

Robey: No known traffic.

Valentich: I am — seems (to) be a large aircraft below five thousand feet.

Robey: What type of aircraft is it?

Valentich: I cannot affirm. It is four bright (sic), it seems to me like landing lights. The aircraft has just passed over me at least a thousand feet above.

The two-way conversation continued:

Valentich: It's approaching right now from due east towards me. [Silence for two seconds] It seems to me he's playing some sort of game. He's flying over me two, three times, at a time, at speeds I could not identify.

Several more questions followed relating to height and description of the mystery craft:

Valentich: It's not an aircraft. It is... [two second silence] ... as it's flying past, it has a long shape [three second silence] it is before me now, Melbourne.

Robey: And how large would the er...the object be?

Valentich: It seems like stationary. What I'm doing now is orbiting and the thing is just orbiting on top of me. It's got a green light and sort of metallic. (like) it's all shiny (on) the outside [five second silence] It's just vanished. Would you know what kind of aircraft I've got? Is it military?

Further transmission contains more questions, answers, confirmations and intentions until:

Valentich: My intentions are to go on to King Island. Ah! Melbourne that strange aircraft is hovering on top of me again [two second silence]. It is hovering and it's not an aircraft, [17 second silence, followed by audible unidentified staccato noise.]

The communication ended at 7:12pm.

Nothing has been discovered that would solve the mystery; if anything the mystery has deepened. Despite an intensive air, land, and sea search no trace of the Cessna was found. An oil slick discovered on October 22, some 29km north of King Island, was found to have no connection with Valentich's plane. Speculation intensified, raising questions of suicide or possibly a staged disappearance. Or even alien attack or abduction? Shot down by drug runners? Electrical discharge from a cloud igniting gas fumes? Or the most plausible cause of disorientation by the pilot? However, none seemed to explain the disappearance or the lights. The more investigators probed the mystery, the more mystifying it appeared.

Frederick Valentich was 22 years old, a rather inexperienced flyer with about 150 total hours flying time and a class-four instrument rating (which meant he could operate at night, but only 'in visual meteorological conditions'). He had twice been rejected by the Royal Australian Air Force, due to inadequate education. Unfortunately, he had failed all five of his exam subjects — not once but twice — and just a month before he disappeared he again failed three subjects. Moreover, the young pilot was enthralled with UFOs, watching films and accumulating articles on the topic. Earlier that year, according to his father, Frederick had told him he had observed a UFO moving very fast and had expressed his worry about what could happen if such presumed extra-terrestrial craft should ever attack.

Adding to the mystery, an amateur photo taken at the time of his disappearance showed a dark unidentifiable shape in the sky. The observer, who wished to remain anonymous, also claimed to have seen a green light just above Valentich's plane on the evening but, fearing ridicule, failed to mention it at the time.

Five years after Valentich's aircraft went missing, an engine cowl flap was found washed ashore on Flinders Island. While not conclusive, the Bureau of Air Safety noted it had come from a Cessna 182 with serial numbers which fell within the range of the aircraft piloted by Frederick Valentich. Its location almost certainly eliminated the theory that he staged his disappearance on the way to King Island.

Based on all the evidence, taken in conjunction with the pilot's own in-flight conversation with air traffic control, there appeared to be sufficient evidence to suggest there was only one outcome, and that had proved fatal for Valentich. However, no explanation has fully determined the nature of the large object with green lights that was said to have accompanied his aircraft during its final descent.

Almost 36 years to the month after Valentich vanished, a South Australian farmer came forward claiming he had seen the missing Cessna around the time it disappeared — it was leaking oil and attached to the side of a UFO. The farmer even took down the plane's registration number but he too failed to come forward, fearing ridicule. For many years the mystery kept resurfacing and as each story sounded more implausible, they continued to haunt Valentich's father who on every anniversary could be seen standing on the coastline staring out to sea in private tribute to his missing son.

Source: Australian Department of Transport

Strange Lights and Crop Circles

In the weeks surrounding the Frederick Valentich disappearance, a series of strange sightings were reported across the Bass Strait coastlines of Tasmania and Victoria. On October 9, 1978, a couple driving the coast road in northern Tasmania reported to police that they had encountered a bright light and mystery object. They described their ordeal which began when the light suddenly appeared above their vehicle. The light then dropped from the sky to the level of their car, maintaining the same speed as their vehicle for some minutes before it suddenly accelerated and disappeared just as mysteriously into the sky above them.

Exactly a month later in Hobart, a taxi driver reported that he was forced to slam on his brakes due to a strange green light in the middle of the road ahead of him. His two-way radio also mysteriously cut out. By the time he had returned his gaze to the road, the green object flew off as quickly as it has appeared.

Two years earlier Tasmania had been gripped by another famous UFO sighting now known as the 'Kettering Incident'. A dome-shaped object was reported to have landed at Little Oyster Cove near Kettering, south of Hobart, in February 1976. A 39-year-old witness described how he had been woken by what he thought was a plane crashing nearby. Still in his dressing gown he headed towards the light. He later described being confronted by "an extraordinary dome-shaped object" about 25 metres down the slope with "windows around the object gave (giving) off a bright light. The exterior looked like aluminium".

Through the three or four windows, he described seeing a tall cylindrical object, which he likened to a ship's compass mounting and "motionless grey shapes inside". As he drew closer he told investigators that he could hear a humming noise, like that of an electric motor. Suddenly the object slowly rose from the ground, still humming, increased its speed, became a dot in the sky and disappeared. The whole incident lasted about seven minutes.

The following morning he discovered the grass on which the object had rested was scorched in a circle. The grass later died but when replaced it became much greener that its surrounding area, adding to the mystery of the 'Kettering Incident'.

The Bruny Island Disappearance

Another unexplained incident linked to strange lights in the sky involved a young woman who went missing from Tasmania's Bruny Island. In March 2011, Rachel Funari disappeared from her island home, leaving behind all of her belongings, including her purse full of money. Police found nothing to indicate she had been planning to leave and immediately launched a widespread land, air and sea search.

That in itself would have been classified as just another missing person case. But as investigations widened, reports began to emerge of strange lights in the sky on the evening in question. Whether or not the lights, or a spate of similar sightings over Tasmania were connected to her disappearance, was and still is an open mystery.

While investigators believed the bulk of strange sightings could be explained away as aircraft, astronomic events or even balloons, they admitted not everything could be explained. But not all UFO mysteries materialised over the Apple Island or the 'Bass Strait Triangle' and unlike most UFO incidents that were never fully explained there is one sighting that was hard to ignore.

The Tully Saucer Nest

The year 1966 was a major one for UFO activity in Australia. Just ask the 200 witnesses to the Westall sighting in Melbourne. What played out at Horseshoe Lagoon on a Queensland farming property has also been described as "an extraordinary testament to the case for UFO reality".

The events began around 9:00am on the morning of January 19, 1966, just weeks before the Westall incident in Melbourne. Farmer George Pedley was driving a tractor on land belonging to his neighbour, banana grower Albert Pennisi. The weather was calm, the morning sun rising in the sky. As his tractor rumbled down the bush track, from beneath the vehicle the banana grower detected a faint hiss. He leant forward to investigate, assuming his tyres had a leak. Just at that moment he claimed, a saucer-shaped object, silvery blue and grey in colour and about seven metres in diameter, rose before him. The object lifted slowly from the nearby lagoon to the height of treetops before tilting slightly and speeding away to the south-west. Pedley claims he ran through the thick reeds and sword grass surrounding the lagoon, forcing his way through the undergrowth until he reached the location from where it had emerged. A large whirlpool had formed, and as the dead reeds below the eddy slowly rose to the surface, it formed a 'nest' revealing a perfect imprint roughly nine meters across in the shape of an inverted saucer.

Two more nests were located hidden in the thick swamp grass, one swirled clockwise and another anticlockwise. By the end of the day investigators and dozens of media who had been alerted had located a total of six nests among the reeds. From that moment on, the term 'saucer nest' left an indelible mark, not only in the Tully swamp, but in the history of the UFO folklore.

Source: State Library Queensland.

Nullarbor Encounter

Reports of UFOs and bright mysterious lights are as varied as the locations where they were purported to have appeared. From South Australia in the year 1988, a family driving through the Nullarbor claimed to have experienced their entire car lifting off the ground. According to their story on local ABC, the Knowles family had been making the long drive from Perth to Melbourne when they were tormented by a large glowing sphere of light for 90 minutes. They described the glowing ball chasing them before landing on the roof and lifting their vehicle "clear off the ground" before dumping them and flying off.

The Cahill Abduction or 'Eumemmering Creek Encounter'

One of the more implausible news reports emerged five years later when a woman driving back to Melbourne from the nearby Dandenong Ranges claimed to have been abducted by aliens in Narre Warren North. According to media reports, it was on a dark winter's night in 1993 when Kelly Cahill and her husband Andrew were driving along the Belgrave-Hallam Road in Narre Warren, on the outskirts of Melbourne. They were on their way to a friend's house when they first saw a row of five or six large orange lights of a "distinct circular shape" in a nearby paddock.

When they arrived at their destination, they all laughed off their encounter, however on their return journey some hours later they spotted the same orange lights hovering above the road before them. They would later describe to disbelieving reporters how the object then flew off "at incredible speed", but a short time later they saw it again in a paddock on the side of the road. Again, they stopped to observe and this time she reported having seen "figures standing behind the portals" of the object. After that, Ms Cahill said her memory of the events blanked out, "like a scene cut from a film".

In the days and weeks that followed, she claimed to find strange marks on her body, including a small triangular wound below her bellybutton and began experiencing stomach pains. Through a series of treatments and hypnosis, she said, she was able to unlock her 'missing time' from that night, describing a tall thin figure with glowing red eyes which appeared in front of the object and emitting a thought message: "Let's kill them." She also revealed more beings appeared, unleashing an energy force that knocked Ms Cahill to the ground as she screamed to her husband, "They've got no souls! They're evil! They're going to kill us!"

Under hypnosis she was also able to recollect another car that night whose occupants had also witnessed the events. A number of women in that second group, who were later located also described similar triangular wounds near their navels, as well as other strange marks. Unlike Kerry Cahill, they refused to go public. Kerry Cahill's recollections were then compiled into a best-selling book, *Encounter*, and featured on local media outlets and the *X-Files* TV series.

A 300 page dossier of those events was later passed onto a UFO organisation but has since disappeared as did Kelly Cahill who reportedly left the country in the late 1990s. As Sydney-based UFO researcher Bill Chalker, lamented, "I used to think this was the holy grail case of encounter reports — I no longer hold that opinion. This was an extraordinary opportunity that we simply lost."

In 2020 Ms Cahill was located by an ABC reporter living in Victoria's Latrobe Valley in Gippsland, the same region she was living in when she and her then husband said they experienced their 'encounter' in 1993. Today she is reluctant to talk about it anymore, leaving others to share their own stories of unexplained phenomena.

Sources: ABC News, *Guardian*, Newscorp

Television and UFOs

If UFO sightings are as frequent as the public is led to believe, why they ask, has a crystal-clear image of a flying saucer not emerged on national television? Extraordinary claims always require extraordinary evidence and in defence of Australian media it has not been for want of trying. If there is one constant in UFO reporting, it's that media coverage tends to be the 'tail that wags the dog', as reporters have historically fuelled the most dramatic UFO mythologies. We are told there are two main types of people who witness UFOs. Smokers and dog watchers — mainly because that group appear to spend the most time outdoors. There are also two types of people who react to UFO stories: believers and sceptics. Invariably the sceptics have the numbers to severely damage reputations and credibility.

Such was a case in 1978 when a former news colleague captured what his television network claimed was "exclusive vision" and a "scoop of all scoops". It was shortly after Frederick Valentich's aircraft mysteriously disappeared after reporting a UFO over Bass Strait. Reporter Quentin Fogarty was on holidays with his family in New Zealand when a pilot of an Argosy cargo plane reported he was being followed by a series of unidentified objects while flying over the Cook Island Straits. The objects were also confirmed on Wellington radar and also sighted by hundreds of people on the ground.

As the mystery surrounding Valentich was still fresh in the mind of the news editor at ATV0 (now Channel 10), he rang Fogarty in New Zealand suggesting he charter a similar flight to reconstruct the events. Which he did. It was on this flight he and his camera crew witnessed the same lights following them, only this time the unidentified objects were being filmed. By the time he arrived back in Melbourne with his exclusive footage the network's publicity department had swung into full gear with a saturation radio campaign promoting the "scoop of all scoops". The problem was when the story went to air the video didn't match the hype. All we saw were tiny dots flickering across the screen. There were no little green men and no shiny flying saucers. The pictures simply didn't meet the expectation of the publicity and the reaction from viewers and sceptics was simply scathing.

In a desperate attempt to salvage some credibility, the film was taken to the USA where Bruce Maccabee, an optical physicist who specialised in laser technology for the US Navy, provided some form of visual authentication. Several months later his results found in all probability they were UFOs. However, it was too late for vindication. My colleague suffered severe stress and subsequently left the industry while the network was forced to hunker down until the story became 'yesterday's news'. Such is the risk to credibility when reporting on unexplained paranormal mysteries whether they are UFOs or crop circles.

Crop Circles
Bamawm, Victoria

On December 4, 1977, word had travelled quickly of a mystery crop circle in central Victoria and we flew to the scene almost as quickly. I arrived with full camera crew from HSV7 Melbourne to find an enterprising farmer had already backed up his tray truck to the edge of the circle, allowing the TV cameras from all the city networks an overview of its symmetrical form.

There it was, just like the others:

August 1977, Leitchville, Victoria

A 13 metre wide circle in the grass appeared on the property of Lloyd Naylor. It was doughnut shaped with a one metre wide band of dried grass around its circumference. The centre was one metre of dead grass.

September 30, 1977, Leitchville, Victoria

Douglas Fehring found a perfect circle of affected grass in his paddock and reported it.

October 21, 1977, Cohuna, Victoria

Four doughnut-shaped circles were located in an irrigated paddock. They were 3 to 3.6 metres in diameter, including a 45 centimetre-wide band of dry withered grass.

December 4, 1977, Leitchville, Victoria

Ken Church discovered a large circular area consisting of a 38 centimetre-wide band around an eight metre diameter circle of chopped clover. There were patches that were reported to have been burnt and appeared as if they had been made by jet engines.

December 1977, Bamawm, Victoria.

So back to my first crop circle in 1977 after farmers John Collins and his brother found a perfect ring 2.4 metres in diameter. What made this report slightly different was a bright light reportedly seen floating above his property the night before discovering the circle.

Crop circles — or agriglyphs — was a phenomenon that began in the 1960s.

The number of crop circles had substantially increased worldwide with many reports concluding they had been created by a force totally at odds with modern science. One British investigator claimed them impossible to have been made by human hand.

After filming the Victorian phenomena, we concluded our interviews, took soil samples for analysis and adjourned to the local pub. Our soil sample was inconclusive although another media source claimed to have found traces of electromagnetic particles from their sample.

Twenty years later, during a casual lunch I was introduced

to a country farmer from central Victoria. He grabbed my hand and with a wry smile said, "We've met before. You came to our farm where me and my brother created a crop circle." Somewhat stunned, I asked him to explain. Unashamedly, he described how he stood in the centre of his field of wheat with a length of string while his brother created a perfect circle around him with a mower. "We then beat the shit around the edges with wet sacks, to give the impression of a mystery force and called the newspapers. Once the story made front page you guys came like a dog to a bone."

Yes, there is always a dilemma facing journalists when it comes to events such as the paranormal.

In June 2021 a report into UFO activity was submitted to the US Congress. The ambiguity of its findings was unable to definitively rule out theories that unidentified phenomena might have been extraterrestrial in nature.

Sources: *Sydney Morning Herald,* Newscorp, Network 7, UFO Researcher Bill Chalker, Victorian State Library, Excerpts from *The Newsman* (Brolga).

Bass Strait
Australia's Bermuda Triangle?

Since maritime records first began, hundreds of vessels, from small yachts to the size of bulk carriers, have come to grief in Australia's notorious Bass Strait. However, those records also include dozens of ships and planes said to have disappeared as mysteriously as those reported lost to the infamous Bermuda Triangle.

Australia's Bermuda Triangle

For decades, the Atlantic Ocean's fabled 'Bermuda Triangle' has been a source of fascination, fear and foreboding. Also known as the 'Devil's Triangle' or 'Hurricane Alley' this notoriously defined region of the North Atlantic is where hundreds of aircraft, ships and people are said to have disappeared under mysterious circumstances. Some believe supernatural forces have been at play. The more extreme theorists have raised the spectre of alien abductions and unseen vortices sucking objects into other dimensions.

On his first voyage to the new world Christopher Columbus reported a huge flame (possibly a meteor) crashing into the sea, then strange lights in the sky weeks later. He also wrote about erratic compass readings, perhaps because it is one of the few places on Earth where true north and magnetic north lined up.

In 1918, the collier *USS Cyclops*, a 165 metre Navy cargo ship with over 300 men onboard, simply disappeared without trace and with no explanation. Some 27 years later an entire squadron of bombers disappeared in the airspace above the Bermuda Triangle and, as in the *Cyclops* incident, there was no explanation given and no wreckage or survivors were found.

Since then, it's estimated that more than 100 ships and planes have vanished in similar strange circumstances, adding to the mystery of the Bermuda Triangle. Here in Australia, Bass Strait, which is a treacherous stretch of water between mainland Australia and Tasmania, has been likened to the Bermuda Triangle with dozens of ships and planes also mysteriously disappearing without trace.

The first report can be traced back to the eighteenth century when the sloop *Eliza* went missing in 1797 on her return voyage to Sydney. She had been searching for another vessel, *Sydney Cove*, which had foundered and sank in the Furneaux group of islands in Bass Strait. Unlike the *Sydney Cove*, *Eliza* left no clues.

From 1838–1840, at least seven vessels and crew were lost on their way to or from new settlements at the time. Rumours abounded that some of these vessels had fallen victim to unscrupulous wreckers or pirates but the most probable cause was bad weather or uncharted reefs. However, lack of wreckage or survivors also raised the questions of mysterious interventions.

In December 1839 whilst on a voyage from Melbourne to Hobart, the 220-tonne barque, *Britomart* with a cargo of livestock, seven passengers and a crew of 23, was lost off Preservation Island, Furneaux Group. Soon after the ship's disappearance, wreckage, personal items, the ship's logbook and compass were reported to have been seen in the possession of the Bass Strait Island's residents. Sealers had more money than usual, and it was said that they had been heard bragging about their knowledge of the wreck. Captain Gill, on the government cutter *Vansittart*, was sent to search for the *Britomart*, and on February 7, 1840 he returned to Launceston with no further information. There were many and varied rumours of foul play including the intentional wrecking and murder of the *Britomart's* crew and passengers, by escaped convicts, pirates or local Indigenous people. And while all 30 people aboard the vessel are believed to have drowned, strong rumours persisted for years that a white woman had survived and was taken in by an Aboriginal community. Despite reports she had been seen in several parts of Gippsland over the next few years, the disappearance was never solved. It just added yet another mystery to the 'Bass Strait Triangle' story. One of the most significant disappearances was that of the British warship *HMS Sappho* in 1858, which disappeared with the loss of over 100 lives and no positively identifiable wreckage located. A similar event took place 12 years later when the *Harlech Castle* disappeared, taking all 23 crew members with her.

In 1920, while sailing into the Bass Strait, the *SS Amelia J* disappeared without a trace shortly after entering the infamous stretch of water. The Australian military conducted an extensive search of the area, then two of the military aircraft involved in the search also vanished. Perhaps strangest about those incidents were reports of strange lights in the skies over the Bass Strait at the time. While this is perhaps the first report of unidentified lights, two other very similar accounts took place in the 1900s.

In 1901, the *SS Federal* vanished without trace along with her 22 crew and, five years later in 1906, the *Ferdinand Fischer*, a German cargo ship, met a similar fate as it made its way to the coast of Tasmania.

In December 1979, the yacht *Charleston*, along with five crew members, vanished without a trace while sailing through Bass Strait. The yacht was scheduled to arrive in Sydney for New Year's Eve. However, after several days with no contact and no arrival, search planes were sent out in a desperate bid to find the apparently stricken vessel. Nothing of the boat or the people on board was ever discovered. There are plenty of theories as to what might have happened, though. Some suggested that, due to an increase in wind around the time the ship disappeared, it was possible that damage could have been inflicted upon the mast, or perhaps a loose container from the many ships passing through the area had damaged the craft. If this was the case, it's possible that the yacht could have drifted as far as islands to the south of New Zealand yet no stress call or radio contact was ever made. The yacht's fate is still a maritime mystery to this day.

In fact, hundreds of vessels from small yachts and fishing craft up to the size of bulk carriers have come to grief in Bass Strait, either hitting uncharted reefs, or foundering due to wild storms. However, like the *Charleston*, dozens more have just mysteriously disappeared without a trace.

Not all mystery disappearances have been confined to shipping. As in the Bermuda Triangle, the Strait has also claimed dozens of aircraft. In 1920 a single-engine bi-plane bomber engaged in the search for the missing schooner *Amelia J* vanished without trace. It was believed to have gone into the sea off the southern coast of Flinders Island but no trace or wreckage was ever found.

In October 1934, while crossing Bass Strait in perfect weather conditions the airliner *Miss Hobart* vanished. There were 11 people on board: nine passengers and two pilots. Neither they nor even the smallest amount of wreckage was ever discovered, despite extensive air and sea searches.

Aviation experts, both at the time and today, believe the loss of the *Miss Hobart* to be a genuine mystery, not least due to the de Havilland DH86 aircraft being one of the most advanced of its time. It had the advantage of four independent engines and the likelihood of all four engines failing at the same time has been almost universally dismissed. The last transmission from the *Miss Hobart* added to the mystery with crew allegedly claiming they could hear the sound of another "aerial machine" coming toward them. They then reported that the humming sound suddenly stopped. Nothing more was heard from the *Miss Hobart* after that.

A year later, a similar aircraft was lost with all on board off Flinders Island and while the cause of both accidents was probably a combination of human error or aircraft design, an air of mystery surrounded the investigations.

During the World War 2 there were no official reports of any enemy fighters entering Bass Strait, yet a large number of aircraft were lost in this stretch of water. Several aircraft — mostly RAAF Bristol Beaufort bombers — were lost during exercises or training flights out of air bases, mainly from Sale in southern Victoria. These accidents were probably caused by inexperienced crew crashing into the sea while performing low-level bombing practice — but to have lost a reported 17 aircraft in one area alone is a mystery in itself.

In 1972, a De Havilland Tiger Moth flown by Brenda Hean and Max Price disappeared on a flight from Tasmania to Canberra as part of protests against the flooding of Lake Pedder in Tasmania. It was believed to have crashed at sea somewhere between the east coast and Flinders Island. But the most famous incident, and the one that has been the inspiration for countless paranormal explanations, involved the disappearance of Frederick Valentich in 1978.

In the next chapter, there is another mystery associated with the treacherous shores of Bass Strait and while it occurred well before my lifetime, I can claim a vague connection.

Sources: Trove, Argus newspapers, *Hobart Town Courier* (Tasmania) Marcus Lowth Australia Broadcasting Corporation: Jack Loney *(1980), Mysteries of the Bass Strait Triangle*, Neptune Press.

Mahogany and Missing Maritime

For a country 'girt by sea' Australia boasts a proud maritime legacy despite mutineers, violent storms, uncharted reefs and ships that disappeared without trace. In the late 1950s I set out to solve one of Australia's great maritime mysteries. But like so many attempts before and since, the fabled Mahogany Ship is still missing.

Search for Mahogany

It was mid-September in 1959. Admittedly I had just turned 16 years of age and what knowledge of Australian maritime history was limited to that of a disinterested Year Nine secondary school student attending Warrnambool High School. At the beginning of that year my father had accepted a new job and as a family we had moved to the Western District of Victoria to live in the picturesque fishing town of Port Fairy. In hindsight I doubt 'picturesque' would even have been in my vocabulary.

Port Fairy was a small town of bluestone cottages, weather beaten shopfronts with leaning verandas stretching above deep and dangerous street gutters. Old-fashioned streetlights hung in loops and swayed in the constant winds that swept up from Bass Strait. In hindsight, it was a quaint town with a significant past waiting to be rediscovered; like one of its mysteries that lay buried nearby beneath the shifting sand dunes along the windswept rip-torn southern coast of Victoria.

My interest in the mystery of Australia's Mahogany Ship began from the back seat of a battered Bedford school bus which rattled each day between Port Fairy and Warrnambool High School.

We would pass the dramatic extinct volcano known as Tower Hill and the nondescript turnoff to the small hamlet of Killarny. There, in the misty distance were the shifting sand dunes where, I was told, the fabled ship lay buried.

It was during the September school holidays that year, together with two recently bonded mates, we set off on our bikes in the hope of discovering its existence. We were guided to the site by a local potato farmer, a relative of one of my new colleagues, whose Irish born great grandfatherr insisted he had seen it, just as many locals in the area claimed to have had family members who swore it existed. As we dug under the watchful eye of the farmer, who even provided the spades, the crashing waves created a mist-like shroud that continually hung over the dunes.

The conditions would not have been too dissimilar to that bleak day in 1836 when three naked sealers trudged along the same coastal beach just after miraculously surviving their own shipwreck ordeal.

Apparently on arriving at the Port Fairy whaling station, they reported they had seen a ship lying intact in the dunes back towards Warrnambool. A detailed description indicated that, instead of the familiar planks, it had wooden panels similar to those found on a Portuguese caravel. This led to speculation that it might have been a ship from the fleet of Portuguese navigator Cristovas de Mendonca who, some time in 1521, sailed to Malacca before heading off into the great unknown.

The earliest documented account of the wreck was carried by a Portland newspaper in 1847 which described "a wreck, about two miles on the Belfast (Port Fairy) side of

Warrnambool…of…a three-hundred-ton vessel …thrown completely into the [sand] hummocks". The article went on to connect the wreck with the discovery of a number of articles of foreign origin found strewn along the beach. Not Portuguese but noting that until the wreck is found, "all theories must remain to some degree speculative".

The description was validated by local residents who regularly visited the site in the latter half of the nineteenth century before it was suddenly covered over by shifting sands following a violent storm, never to be seen again.

Another theory is that the Mahogany Ship was an incomplete vessel probably built by escaped Tasmanian convicts. It could have also been the schooner *Unity* in 1813, which was wrecked or beached nearby. While there is no conclusive evidence such a wreck exists today, nineteenth century accounts of the relic persist both in popular folklore and in many academic publications from the time. In more recent years documented accounts have surfaced from purported nineteenth century eyewitnesses to the wreck. Yet the Mahogany Ship itself remains hidden.

After several hours of digging, boredom settled in and so we handed back our spades before returning to Port Fairy and the simple pleasures of riding the disused railway on Griffiths Island at the mouth of the Moyne River. Built in 1855 to service the Port Fairy lighthouse, it too had succumbed to time and, like much of the area's history, it lay partly buried just beneath the surface. In 1999 and again in 2004 I took more than a passing interest as a newsman reporting that sonar detectors and heavy drilling equipment had been brought in to try and locate this fabled vessel. However, like our dig 50 years earlier, they too failed and so the Mahogany Ship and the mystery that unfolded in 1836 continues to this day.

While the Mahogany Ship left a legacy if not a tangible

sign of its once existence, there is a far more tragic maritime legacy around Australia — of vessels that simply disappeared without trace.

The *Batavia*

For almost 400 years one of the most baffling and brutal maritime mysteries of all time lay buried near a mass grave and a rotting hulk, just off the coast of West Australia. In 1628, the *Batavia* was the largest ship built by the biggest company in the world, the Dutch East India Company. Filled full of treasure, a plot to mutiny began fermenting during its maiden voyage from New Holland to Batavia (now Jakarta), Indonesia.

Then on June 4, 1629, before the mutineers had time to muster, the *Batavia* sank 60km off the West Australian coast. As the ship broke apart, 40 of the 341 passengers drowned while the remainder, including men women and children, scrambled ashore on a group of small, deserted islands.

After the commander and captain took the only boat large enough to sail the remaining 3,000km voyage to Batavia to raise the alarm, the leadership fell to Jeronimus Cornelisz, a master manipulator intent on carrying out his brutal mutiny. Over the course of several weeks, he slaughtered approximately 125 of the survivors, including women and children, although a small number of women were kept as sex slaves.

However, some of the men who had been sent away in search of water returned to discover the slaughter and began a series of pitched battles against the mutineers. In October, at the height of their last and deadliest fight, they were joined by the return of the *Batavia*'s commander. Leaders of the mutineers were subsequently overpowered, tried and convicted, becoming the first Europeans to be legally executed on what is now Australian territory.

The wreck site was first discovered in 1963 and a mass grave was found on Beacon Island in 1999. Only then did police and maritime experts, using modern forensic science begin to unravel *Batavia's* long forgotten mystery and lay to rest the wretched souls buried without trace just off the Australian coast almost 400 years ago.

The *Waratah*: Australia's *Titanic*

The *Waratah*, sometimes referred to as 'Australia's Titanic', was a 500-foot (153m) steamer and like the *Titanic*, was considered unsinkable. Its passengers enjoyed similar luxury features to the *Titanic* with saloons, cabins with smoking rooms and even special areas set aside for women and children. After leaving Adelaide on July 7, 1909 *Waratah* arrived a day ahead of schedule in Durban, South Africa where it unloaded some of the cargo and took on more passengers adding to the 82 already on board, including many from Sydney, Melbourne and Adelaide. Refuelling with coal for the remainder of the voyage, it was now running slightly behind schedule but left Durban confident of making up time on route to Cape Town before continuing on to London.

The last possible sighting of *Waratah* by the *Guelph* was on the night of July 27 and, while running late, there were no signs of it flying any signals of distress. But the unthinkable happened. The unsinkable *Waratah* mysteriously disappeared without trace.

As news gradually reached Australia the Chair of the House of Representatives noted that "great anxiety began sweeping the nation" as loved ones hung on to hope that it was adrift somewhere waiting to be rescued. Horrified authorities quickly ordered a search but after three months nothing was found. A second, much larger and longer search was commissioned including many ships, but none sighted the *Waratah* or found any wreckage.

Suddenly on August 14 it was reported by the Blue Anchor Line that the ship had been found and for a short time "bells sounded amid much rejoicing and relief". But the joy would be short lived as the truth revealed it to be nothing more than a very cruel unconfirmed rumour. Even so, the London owners of the *Waratah* still believed it was afloat and probably drifting towards Australia.

In early September the Admiralty in London refused to deploy any warships to search for the *Waratah* as up to 15 steamers were already still in the area. Slowly Australia was forced to come to terms with the reality it was lost.

Today, more than 100 years later, the mystery continues to baffle maritime experts, spawning many conspiracy theories and yet even with expensive modern-day underwater sonar equipment searches have failed to find any trace of it. The unsinkable *Waratah* simply disappeared with 211 passengers aboard remaining one of Australia's most baffling nautical mysteries of all time.

The *Zuytdorp*

On August 1, 1711 the *Zuytdorp* (meaning 'south village') was dispatched from the Netherlands. It was reported to be holding a load of freshly minted silver coins to take to the trading port of Batavia, now Jakarta, Indonesia. It never arrived at its destination. No search was undertaken since there was no idea where the ship was lost. The crew was never heard from again. In 1834, Aboriginal people near the recently colonised settlement of Perth reported wreckage and coins on the beach some distance to the north. Local officials assumed it was a recent wreck and having sent rescue parties which failed to find any survivors or their remains, the search was soon abandoned.

In 1927 more wreckage was again discovered at the foot of cliffs around the same location. This time, coins (some dated 1711), bottle fragments, timbers including a spar, a carved female figure, breech blocks from swivel guns and other objects, including evidence of a deliberately lit fire, were found.

Drawing from the previous report authorities believed the relics strongly pointed to the *Zuytdorp* which disappeared without trace off the WA coast in 1711 with the loss of all 286 lives.

The *Madagascar*

The mystery of the *Madagascar* in 1853 raised as much interest and speculation as the discovery of the *Mary Celeste* 19 years later, when it was found drifting, abandoned and with no sign of life and no indication of what had happened.

The *Madagascar*, a large British merchant ship, arrived in Melbourne from Plymouth after 87 days at sea carrying cargo, passengers and a crew of 60. Fourteen crew members then jumped ship to head for the gold diggings. After signing up replacement crew members it then loaded its cargo, including two tons of gold, for the return journey.

On Wednesday August 10, just as it was preparing to sail, police boarded the ship and arrested bushranger John Francis, who was wanted for his involvement in the McIvor goldfield robbery several weeks earlier. There had already been a hold-up on the St Kilda and Brighton Road around that time, as well as an audacious robbery of gold bullion from the barque *Nelson*, then moored at Williamstown in readiness to sail. Although three men were arrested, the *Nelson* gold was never recovered so police were determined to prevent a similar robbery.

On the following day police arrested two others, one on board the ship and the other as he was preparing to board. As a result of these arrests, *Madagascar* did not leave Melbourne until Friday August 12, 1853. After clearing Port Phillip Heads the *Madagascar* turned left and was never seen again. While there was much speculation as to what happened, including a mutiny by renegade crew members, no wreckage, no survivors and no gold was ever found.

Missing Sub *HMAS AE1*

Submarine *HMAS AE1* had only been in Sydney for two days in 1914 when news came through that Serbia had disregarded an ultimatum from Austria and that war was imminent. Just a few months later, Britain and Germany declared war and Australia had no choice but to enter the conflict.

HMAS AE1 and other warships were mobilised and set sail up the Queensland coast bound for Rabaul, Papua New Guinea. Once the submarine arrived on September 14 she joined the destroyer *Parramatta* for a patrol of Cape Gazelle. Both ships were to stay within viewing range of each other to ensure they re-entered the harbour before nightfall. At some point in the mid-afternoon, *Parramatta* lost sight of the sub. When by 8:00pm *HMAS AE1* still hadn't returned or been heard from, a search was launched. Theories ranged from a German attack to a mechanical breakdown causing the submarine to be swept out to the open sea, and even an internal explosion. The submarine has never been found.

1988: *Patanela*

While the iconic tale of the *Mary Celeste* is still one of the most enduring and puzzling events to unfold on the high seas, the *Patanela* has become the Australian equivalent to that maritime mystery.

The 19 metre steel-hulled *Patanela* left Fremantle, West Australia in early October 1988, bound for Airlie Beach in Queensland, to begin a new life as a charter vessel. It was last seen under full sail making solid progress towards the New South Wales coast and its ultimate destination.

Then on November 8 the *Patanela* vanished while passing Sydney with all four people aboard. There was no rough weather at the time and the ship was fitted out with the latest navigational, communications and safety equipment. No mayday call was received and no distress flares were sighted. No debris nor bodies turned up; the *Patanela* simply vanished without a trace.

Almost 20 years after the ship's disappearance, a couple on a beach at Eucla, near the border between West Australia and South Australia, found a handwritten message in a bottle dated just a week or two before the disappearance:

Hi there. Out here in the lonely Southern Ocean and thought we would give away a free holiday in the Whitsunday Islands in north Queensland, Australia. Our ship is travelling from Fremantle, to Queensland to work as a charter vessel.

The only other trace of the *Patanela* was a barnacle-encrusted lifebuoy found floating off Terrigal almost seven months after the disappearance. Over the years there have been numerous rumoured sightings, leading to theories of hijacking and foul play, but nothing was ever confirmed and the fate of the *Patanela* and its crew still remains one of Australia's unsolved maritime mysteries.

Jian Seng

In 2006, an Australian coast watch plane found a ship floating 180 km south-west of Weipa, Queensland in the Gulf of Carpentaria. Not unlike the *Mary Celeste* there was no explanation as to why it was empty. It had just a broken toe line hanging from its bow. All the investigators could go on was its name *Jian Seng* printed on the side, but there was nothing else to identify the ship. Investigations found no records of distress signals, no identifying documents or belongings, and no reports of any missing boat matching that description. Officials have never been able to determine who it belonged to or where it came from. Just another lasting maritime mystery.

Sources: WA Museum, South African History online, *Illawarra Mercury, Sydney Morning Herald.*

Lost, Missing or Murdered?

In Australia, more than 38,000 people are reported missing each year. While most are found within a short period of time, approximately 2,600 are deemed long term missing persons; even many of those are eventually located. Then there are those who are never seen again. Where there is no body or remains discovered, there is no closure and with no closure the pain of loss and uncertainty can last a lifetime for their families.

A Personal Mystery

Eloise Worledge

7:30am on Monday, January 12, 1976

The slightly built four-year-old boy padded barefoot down the hallway into his parents' bedroom, as he did most mornings. He slipped between their sheets and as he curled up between them, Blake Worledge uttered the six short words that would trigger his parents' worst nightmare, "Ella is not in her bed." His sister, eight-year-old Eloise Worledge, had been abducted from her home in the middle of the night. Despite the state's biggest missing person search and a $10,000 reward, she was never found.

One week after Eloise Worledge was reported missing I was sent to their family home in the Melbourne bayside suburb of Beaumaris in the hope of filming the first one-on-one interview with her devastated mother, Patsy. HSV7 news editor John Maher was convinced it was a domestic dispute. "Daughters don't just disappear. Get inside that house. Use your bloody charm," he said. "Find out what happened."

The damp smell of tea tree hung in the air from the light morning drizzle as I walked the short path to the front door. An overturned tricycle on the front lawn lay as a symbol of happy family times but added to the impending moment of intrusion I was about to impose on the parents — the moment most journalists dread.

I knocked. I waited. A moment later the door suddenly swung open. "I am so terribly sorry to intrude ..."

"I know who you are, Mal. Please come in."

Within minutes Patsy Worledge was fussing around in her kitchen, organising coffee for the crew who had now joined me in the lounge and were rearranging furniture for the interview. Lindsay Worledge was not present and Patsy made no apology. In fact, I felt some relief as his rather brusque and somewhat defensive nature had reportedly intimidated some senior police who had placed him as the main suspect. Police who received the initial phone call recorded Lindsay Worledge telling them in an unemotional and almost off-hand tone that there had been a break-in at his house and "the only thing missing is my eight-year-old daughter".

Panic-stricken, Patsy first rang her sister and then ran across the road to a neighbour. I asked if she suspected anyone without specifically naming her husband. But she replied no, and then quickly followed up saying she fully believed that Eloise would soon be returned. This supported the initial theory that her husband may have been involved as retribution to their impending separation and that, after a brief period, Eloise would be returned. Patsy also elaborated on how the fly-wire screen had been cut from inside the home and how police had discovered traces of tan bark on the bedroom floor from the garden bed below the open window. It was believed Eloise and her abductor left through the front door.

Our interview suddenly took on an edge as Patsy voiced frustration that police had not taken the abduction seriously at first, treating it as a domestic. She accused junior police, who initially responded to their call, of being incompetent in that they had trampled over vital evidence beneath Eloise's bedroom window. She then spoke of the huge support from senior police who had formed a special task force within days, headed by Detective Superintendent Fred Warnock. I also took copious notes concentrating on names Patsy referred to, including her close friend Pauline. It was Pauline who was among the first to support the family on hearing of Eloise's disappearance. It was with Pauline that she had shared her initial grief and suspicions. Pauline, I noted, would become someone to contact later should this interview become the basis of an extended program.

Several months later my news editor John Maher appointed a new secretary, a unit manager who would virtually run the news department's management structure. She was classy and efficient, did not suffer fools gladly and, above all, had a great sense of humour. These were the ingredients needed to work alongside Maher in a roomful of hedonistic male egos and females battling for equal rights. She walked straight up to me on her first day in the office, held out her hand and introduced herself. "I'm Pauline, friend of Patsy's." What I didn't know at the time was that Pauline had not only become my boss's secretary but would also become my wife. Patsy Worledge would become godmother to our daughter Sarah and so our lives would become forever linked.

Then on a cold and wet winter's night in August 1997, Patsy's 26-year-old son Blake Worledge left a party and stepped out on to Whitehorse Road in Nunawading straight into the path of an oncoming car. Blake was killed instantly, devastating his surviving family and our wide circle of friends. Once again, we all gathered to offer what support and comfort we could. At the funeral I embraced Blake's father Lindsay and felt his body shudder in inconsolable grief. I remembered at the time of Eloise's disappearance, Detective Superintendent Warnock telling a cynical media that he believed Lindsay Worledge had been unfairly judged. As we stood in that cold damp morning at the Springvale Crematorium I looked into the eyes of a father who had now lost his second child and, like his former wife Patsy, their grief was overwhelming.

Twenty-seven years after Eloise Worledge was snatched from her bed in the dead of night a new investigation was conducted by the Victoria Police Cold Case Unit. Detective Senior Constable Robert Nazaretian told the Melbourne Coroner's Court that despite Eloise's father Lindsay being the prime suspect at the time of her disappearance, the investigation found no new evidence to implicate either of Eloise's parents.

Convicted sex offenders were interviewed when the case was reopened, including a teacher and a librarian at Beaumaris Primary School, as well as a man who coached at the Beaumaris Junior Soccer Club. Police failed to link them to Eloise's disappearance or uncover any evidence linking known sex killer and suspect Raymond 'Mr Stinky' Edmunds to the crime.

Handing down an open finding, Coroner Frank Hender said Eloise Worledge was a shy girl who would not have voluntarily left her home with a stranger. He said significant information given to police included a neighbour's account of hearing a child cry out and a car door slam at 2:00 am on the night of the disappearance. He ruled it impossible to identify who was responsible for Eloise's disappearance. Outside court, Patsy told reporters that the family had been "devoted to learning from our experiences, to healing and accepting the mystery and now we don't actually need to know". Patsy said the family had found its own form of closure years earlier. The case had a lasting impact on my life.

In February 2022 family and friends of Patsy Worledge gathered for her funeral not far from the aged care centre in Brighton, Victoria where she had lived with her second husband Des. We were invited to wear bright colours to represent her vibrancy, her creativity and above all her resilience to life. As she told me many times, "You never get over tragedy. You have to live through it." Patsy Worledge was 79.

Mr Cruel

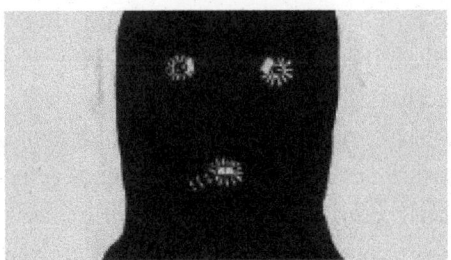

The hood of Mr Cruel.

In the period between 1989 and 1992 Melbourne families were living in fear of a brutal serial sex attacker who was targeting unsuspecting homes, then abducting and abusing innocent children. The Melbourne *Herald Sun* dubbed him 'Mr Cruel' and the rest of us in the media simply followed suit.

It wasn't until the disappearance of 13-year-old Karmein Chan in 1992 (later found murdered) that his reign of terror suddenly ceased. By then it was personal.

I clearly remember the night I arrived home in time to tuck our seven-year-old twins into their beds. As I scooped my hands beneath the pillow of our daughter to kiss her goodnight, I felt the knife. A broad bladed, bone-handled butter knife. "What's this?", I asked. With a mixture of guilt and defiance she replied, "It's in case Mr Cruel comes". This was the moment I realised the impact his reign of terror was having in family homes around Melbourne. Sadly, I also felt a wave of guilt by inflaming this fear on our nightly news. But by now police were needing all the public help and awareness the media could muster.

The first report filtered through the news desk at Network Ten on the morning of August 22, 1987. A violent intruder, masked and armed with a gun and knife, had burst into a family home in the quiet outer suburb of Lower Plenty. He subsequently forced both parents onto their stomachs, bound their hands and feet, before locking them in a closet. He then tied their seven-year-old son to a bed then attacked and abused their 11-year-old daughter. It was over a year later when Mr Cruel struck again and his *modus operandi* appeared to have become bolder and more terrifying.

Just days after Christmas in 1988, John Wills, his wife, and their four daughters were fast asleep in their suburban home, not far from his last attack. As before, with a gun in one hand and wielding a knife in the other, the intruder, wearing dark blue overalls and a blue ski mask, forced the parents to roll onto their stomachs, before they were bound and gagged. Waking their 10-year-old daughter

Sharon Wills by calling her name, he quickly blindfolded and gagged her, before fleeing with his young, terrified hostage. It was just after midnight the following night when a woman stumbled upon Sharon Wills standing on a street corner dressed in green garbage bags. She had not only been washed but Mr Cruel had methodically clipped her fingernails and toenails and brushed and flossed her teeth to remove any forensic evidence.

Mr Cruel struck a third time on July 3, 1990, in the suburb of Canterbury — within the same region of his previous attacks and armed with his usual gun and knife. Parents Brian and Rosemary Lynas were attending a farewell party and had left their two daughters home alone. 15-year-old Fiona and 13-year-old Nicola were woken to a real-life nightmare. Just 20 minutes after the abduction, Brian and Rosemary Lynas returned back home to find 15-year-old Fiona tied to her bed with a ransom message demanding $25,000 for Nicola's return.

A few days later, Nicola was dropped off not far from her home, fully dressed, wrapped in a blanket, and still blindfolded. Only some details of her ordeal were revealed but it became known that she was forced to lay in a neck brace contraption fastened to the abductor's bed, restraining her while she was abused.

The reign of terror would only get worse. On April 13, 1991, Mr Cruel broke into the home of John and Phyllis Chan in the affluent suburb of Templestowe in Melbourne. Thirteen-year-old Karmein was at home babysitting her two younger sisters while both her parents worked at a Chinese restaurant they owned in nearby Eltham. The girls were suddenly confronted by a masked man wielding a large knife, his face completely covered by a black balaclava with white stitching around the eyes and mouth. After forcing Karmein's sisters into a cupboard and barricading them inside he then dragged his teenage victim through the garden gate and out onto the street.

Investigators found a note written in large, bold letters on Phyllis Chan's Toyota Camry. It read, "Pay back, Asian drug dealer. More. More to come." But after combing John Chan's background, this proved to be just another of Mr Cruel's false clues to confuse police. There were no drug deals involving the Chans.

Karmein Chan's abduction triggered one of the largest searches in Australian history, known as Operation Spectrum. Sadly, Karmein would never be reunited with her family. Nearly one year after her abduction, a man walking his dog in nearby Thomastown, discovered a fully decomposed skeleton. The victim, who had been shot several times in the back of her head, was eventually identified as Karmein Chan. There would be no known further attacks attributed to the so-called Mr Cruel leaving a trail of heartbreak and many theories as to his fate.

While the abduction and murder of Karmein Chan may have been his last offence, some police believed that, wracked with guilt, he may have taken his own life. Operation Spectrum lasted for the next few years resulting in 27,000 suspects being questioned and 70 people charged with child pornography. But no leads in the hunt for Mr Cruel.

In 2010, police launched a new investigation hoping that modern forensics may bring an answer that prior detectives had failed to find. Unfortunately, they discovered many of the case files had been misfiled, disorganised, or were just plain missing. One of the vital pieces of DNA evidence — a piece of tape used to bind one of his victims — had disappeared while in police custody. One key suspect, Robert Knight, who had a history of crimes against children was detained in 2013. He eventually pleaded guilty to a series of charges but while awaiting trial, he leaped to his death from the second storey of his prison.

As of this moment, the Mr Cruel case is still unsolved with a reward of over $1 million. As Mr Cruel faded from the news headlines and family life began returning to normal, in one Melbourne home, a bone-handled broad-bladed butter knife had returned to its rightful place in the kitchen drawer.

Cold cases

- Perhaps Australia's most quintessential missing person case — the one that 'broke our innocence' — occurred on Australia Day, 1966 when the three Beaumont children, Jane, Arnna, and Grant were last seen catching a bus to Glenelg Beach near Adelaide, South Australia.
- In a case as sad as it was mysterious, Adelaide was rocked again when Joanne Ratcliff and Kirstie Gordon both went missing on August 25, 1973 from the Adelaide Oval.
- On Boxing Day 1982 10-year-old Bradford Pholi was last seen leaving the family home in Dundas, New South Wales intending to catch a train to Newtown to see his aunt. He never arrived.
- Sarah MacDiarmid caught a train home in July, 1990 after playing tennis with friends. She was travelling from East Melbourne back to Kananook railway station where she had left her vehicle when she disappeared and was never seen again.
- South Australians were again shocked by the disappearance of 12-year-old Rhianna Barreau who disappeared in October, 1992 while walking to her local mall to buy a postcard for her penpal in the USA.
- One year later nine-year-old Craig Ewen Taylor disappeared from a family holiday shack in Coningham, Tasmania, never to be seen again.

• Twelve-year-old Quanne Diec was last seen by her dad on July 27, 1998 as she left her home in Granville, New South Wales on her way to school. Twelve years later, a man was charged but a jury found him not guilty.
• Three-year-old William Tyrell, last seen wearing a Spiderman suit, disappeared without trace from his grandparents' front yard in Kendall, New South Wales on December 12, 2014.

A Missing Prime Minister

Harold Holt

In 1967 Ronald Ryan became the last person hanged in Australia. Sydney had been rocked by a series of brutal underworld killings, while raging bushfires devastated much of Hobart and surrounding areas. But on the seventeenth day of summer, one week before Christmas, Australia was left stunned by one of the biggest stories in its history, if not one of the most baffling mysteries of our time.

Shortly before reading the midday news on Melbourne's Radio 3DB, my main story was being thrown into doubt. A northerly wind sweeping down along the southern coast had delayed the arrival of lone British yachtsman Alec Rose who was due to complete his around the world solo voyage in his tiny yacht *Lively Lady*.

At the end of the bulletin I wandered out through the adjoining newsroom where the only person on duty was a young cadet journalist named Norm Beaman. Phone held to his ear, he placed his forefinger across his lips to indicate he couldn't speak. That phone call was the first dramatic alert from a source in Canberra indicating the Prime Minister of Australia may be missing! No further details were available. Given the nature of the call he immediately rang the news desk of the giant *Herald* newspaper complex four floors above. Within minutes the unbelievable news began to unfold. The Prime Minister of Australia Harold Holt was missing feared drowned.

As the dramatic events unfolded I was seconded into our associated television newsroom at HSV7 where we covered the massive search and rescue operation being conducted at Cheviot Beach on the southern tip of Victoria's Mornington Peninsula.

Each network called in their senior presenters, while reporters rushed to the scene. Channel Seven's David Johnston was already in the area covering the arrival of yachtsman Alec Rose. In fact, of all journalists that day, Johnston was the closest to Cheviot Beach. Had he not been so violently ill in the bottom of the fishing boat he had chartered to cover the arrival of Rose he could have watched the PM several hundred metres away as he waded out into the surf, never to be seen again.

There were many conspiracy theories raised over succeeding years including one involving the PM as a spy who had been plucked from the water by a Chinese submarine. Another theory had the PM swimming around to the next bay where a secret woman admirer met him and they both drove off to spend their lives together elsewhere. There was even talk of suicide. However, the general consensus was that he swam out into the extremely rough waters at

Cheviot Beach in an act of bravado, which ended when the roaring surf collaborated with the surging kelp, dragging him under to become the 67th drowning victim of the year. The media frenzy lasted weeks, however the last word on that first night has since become media folklore. With all the reverence he could muster Channel Seven's host Geoff Raymond finally summed up the historic but tragic day, announcing the search for the missing PM had been called off for the night "after coming to a dead halt".

Juanita Neilson

Mystery still surrounds the 1975 disappearance of Sydney heiress Juanita Nielsen. Or more to the point, who killed her? Nielsen was the feisty 37-year-old journalist/publisher of a Kings Cross newspaper *NOW*, and heiress to the Mark Foy family fortune. On July 4, 1975 she was last seen at the Carousel nightclub, a sleazy hangout for drag queens formerly known as Les Girls. Run by Jim Anderson, an associate of notorious underworld figure Abe Saffron, she arrived slightly hungover and running late for a meeting to discuss advertising in her newspaper. Juanita Neilson then disappeared.

On July 12 her handbag and several personal effects were found abandoned on a freeway towards the Blue Mountains in Sydney's west. But her body has never been found. Many theories abound on what became of Juanita Neilson. Amongst a list of theories, some say she was shot in the head in the stairwell of the Carousel clubrooms; she was strangled and dismembered; or her body was buried under an airport runway, in concrete building foundations or under sand dunes.

Investigations have since revealed just how much of the '70s was an era of corrupt police, politicians and property developers. Nielsen had become a fervent and high-profile campaigner waging a battle against bulldozing heritage buildings in order to build modern apartments. She used her paper to advocate for the preservation of the houses while the Builders Labourers Federation, led by Jack Mundey, put a green ban on the precinct.

Their nemesis was property developer Frank Theeman, who was financially haemorrhaging as a result of their actions. Residents of the disputed homes claimed they were regularly harassed by men employed by Theeman, as he attempted to have them forcibly evicted. A plot was also revealed to kidnap Nielsen four days prior to her Carousel meeting. Three men were arrested and charged with conspiracy to kidnap and two were subsequently convicted, however no charges were ever laid over her disappearance.

It wasn't until November 10, 1983 that a coroner and jury of six declared that Neilson had died "on or shortly after July 4, 1975". They were unable to name the place, the manner or cause of death. A subsequent parliamentary committee investigating her disappearance concluded that corruption had hampered the police investigation. In 1994 the Commonwealth Parliamentary Joint Committee on the National Crime Authority further castigated police ineptitude in the case.

On July 4, 2021, the 45th anniversary of Juanita Nielsen's mysterious disappearance, the New South

Wales government finally offered a $1 million reward in the hope of flushing out those involved. However, most of the key witnesses including two suspects who were convicted of conspiracy to murder, but not for killing her, have since died.

While keen to distance themselves from past corruption, police pledged to explore every line of inquiry and lay to rest the perception that the unsolved mystery of Juanita Nielsen was never properly investigated in the first place. Similar allegations of corruption and incompetence surrounded another tragic mystery of the '70s.

Luna Park Ghost Train Fire

Godson family photo

In June 1979, the Godson family from the small New South Wales town of Warren excitedly packed their car and set out for a much anticipated holiday in Sydney. Parents Jenny and Gordon, with sons Damien (6) and Craig (5) were a long-standing well-respected family in their community. Jenny had once described her husband as being "good, kind, strong and reliable (of) great integrity and lived for his family". John had recently taken on additional work delivering petrol around the countryside and had felt a holiday was one way of compensating his family for his extended hours away from home. As New South Wales was in the grip of a railway strike, travelling was difficult and they arrived late at the Sydney home of their hosts, the Harris's. They soon settled in and their first few days were spent visiting the normal tourist attractions Sydney had to offer.

Their last day, June 9, was spent at Taronga Zoo, before the culmination and highlight of their holiday, a trip to Luna Park. While they waited for a ferry from Circular Quay, a satanic-looking figure approached them dressed in a loin cloth, horned headdress and mask. This strange looking character then placed his hand on six-year-old Damien Godson's shoulder which was captured on camera by the bemused family. Their bemusement would soon turn to horror.

Jenny would later recall their final moments together spending several hours enjoying the various attractions. "It was nearly time for us to leave when the boys asked John if they could have another ride on the Ghost Train and the River Caves. He agreed so I went to get an ice cream and wait."

Godson and the boys boarded their carriage and passed through Hell's Doorway into the twisting corridors of the Ghost Train. After wandering off to buy her ice-cream Jenny suddenly heard screaming and turned to see smoke billowing from the Ghost Train tunnel. As the first car emerged through the door all she remembered seeing was a four-foot wall flames engulfing the tunnel behind it. Emergency Services rushed to the scene, but due to water supply issues, it took longer than expected to get the blaze under control.

Around 35 people were believed to have been on the ride when thick smoke began to escape from the tunnel doors. Staff raised the alarm and began frantically pulling people from the ride as their cars exited the tunnel. It was initially thought that everybody had safely escaped, but at around 11:30pm, the bodies of seven people were found. John Godson and his two children, Damien and Craig, were found huddled together in each other's arms as they sought shelter. The bodies of four Waverley College students, Jonathan Billings, Richard Carroll, Michael Johnson, and Seamus Rahilly were also discovered.

All the ghost-like images from inside that ride had been destroyed including the same demonic figure with the horns resembling the legendary Moloch photographed with his arm on Daniel Godson's shoulder earlier that evening. According to mythology Moloch is said to have preferred children to be burned alive as sacrifices. It was this image captured on the family camera earlier in the evening that left Jenny Godson convinced that some evil force had been present that terrible night. In hindsight there may well have been an evil force involved in the Luna Park Ghost Train fire. There have always been suggestions of suspected arson.

Just hours after the fire had been extinguished, Inspector Doug Knight quickly shut down that speculation concluding instead the fire was caused by an electrical fault. Evidence he said initially supported his finding. However former Luna Park staff described the ride as "running like clockwork with no history of fire trouble at the time".

Persistent allegations circulated in the 1980s that the Ghost Train fire had been deliberately lit at the instigation of entrepreneurs who wanted to redevelop the prime harbour site. In 1987 the National Crime Authority described the original police investigation as "inadequate" and the coronial inquest "ineffective", by failing to discover the true cause of the fire.

In 2007, new evidence was published linking Detective Inspector Doug Knight to a business relationship with an associate of the alleged crime boss Abe Saffron, but failed to establish that Saffron was involved. It was also scathing of the original police investigation.

In 2021, almost 42 years after that tragic event, an ABC investigative team raised a number of serious issues including arson, a coverup involving senior police and political forces at the highest level. During their investigation a number of witnesses who were present on that tragic night, but were never called to give evidence, finally described a distinct smell of accelerant in the immediate aftermath of the fire.

Also speaking publicly for the first time, the prosecutor assisting the inquest slammed the detective in charge of the investigation, describing his conduct as "criminal". Colin Wedderburn now says he believes the fire *was* deliberately lit and that justice had not been done.

In July 2021 the New South Wales government finally posted a $1 million reward for information about the deadly Luna Park Ghost Train fire, even if it did not lead to a charge or conviction. Survivors, families and relatives welcomed the reward saying all they want is closure so the ghosts of Luna Park could finally rest in peace.

As in all unsolved cases, long after the headlines fade the pain continues. And when there is no closure, the pain for the families of victims can become a life sentence. There are currently more than 40 outstanding cold cases on police files still waiting for closure. One of those cases involves a man whose body was found but his identity is still missing, creating one of the most baffling mysteries in Australia's history.

The Somerton Man

In December of 1948, the body of a man was found on Somerton Beach in Adelaide, South Australia. The man had no identification and all the labels on his clothes had been removed. The man had no visible injuries or wounds and as the investigation unfolded, the evidence police uncovered raised more questions than answers.

Investigators theorised that the man must have died from a type of poison as he had no visible wounds. The case seemed unsolvable until police found a tiny scrap of paper rolled tightly and sewn into the waistband of the man's pants. The piece of paper was torn from a book and had the words 'Tamam Shud' (a Persian phrase meaning 'it's finished') printed on it.

Days later a local businessman came forward and handed police a book which he said was thrown through the open window of his car. When police opened the book they found the final page where the words Tamam Shud should have been, was missing. They also discovered two more clues written on the back of the book: a sequence of letters — believed to be a code — and at least one phone number. One of the numbers belonged to a nurse, who denied knowing the victim but allegedly acted strangely when she was shown an impression of the man. Derek Abbott, an engineering professor from the University of Adelaide, who has spent years trying to solve the mystery of the Somerton Man, believes the nurse had a child by the man, though this is yet to be proven.

The codes found on the back of the book have never been cracked, but many have theorised the case is closely related to spies and secret agents. To this day, the story of the Somerton Man is still one of the country's most baffling cold cases.

In May 2021 his body was finally exhumed from a resting place in Adelaide's West Terrace Cemetery. Police conducting the exhumation at the grave found an identification tag confirming the remains of the body found on an Adelaide beach 73 years ago. They said they were optimistic about the prospects of recovering DNA and finally solving the identity of the victim known only as the Somerton Man.

The Man on the Crucifix

In 1994 fisherman Mark Peterson thought he'd snagged the catch of his life when something tugged on his fishing line while out on the Hawkesbury River in New South Wales. Unfortunately, what he pulled from the water was far from aquatic. Peterson had pulled to the surface a heavy piece of steel in the shape of a crucifix, with the remains of a person attached. He immediately called the police who later confirmed they were the remains of a man between the ages of 21 and 41. The bones were anatomically arranged on the crucifix and the victim's entire body was wrapped in plastic and wire. Water had eroded the man's fingerprints, making identification impossible.

He was dubbed 'Rack Man' and lay unclaimed in the morgue until 2018 when he was finally identified as 37-year-old Sydney man Max Tancevski. Experts are still puzzled by the unusual circumstances surrounding his death. Police say the killing was unlikely to be gang or underworld related, instead hypothesising the involvement of a religious or satanic group. They believed the welding on the frame suggested premeditation and that it could be the work of a serial killer — fearing more victims could still be found.

Missing plane

On the night of August 9, 1981, a single-engine Cessna disappeared over the Barrington Tops National Park in New South Wales. Four close friends had chartered the plane to fly them home to Sydney after a holiday on the Whitsundays. At the controls was Mike Hutchins, an ex-RAAF and licensed senior commercial pilot with 3,412 hours experience. Through radio contact with the pilot, it was determined that two vital pieces of equipment had failed and the plane was reacting erratically.

"Our standby compass is swinging like blazes…just to compound things, we thought we had a cockpit fire, but we seem to have resolved that little problem."

As the operator at Sydney Air Traffic Control was warning that 6000 feet was "the lowest safe" height an aircraft can fly in that area, the pilot's voice became noticeably more panicked.

"Mike Delta X-Ray…5000," he yelled. The radio then cut out.

An initial nine-day search involving helicopters and hundreds of volunteers on foot turned up nothing, as did a follow-up search four weeks later with over 400 army reserve members, police officers and bush rescue volunteers. That was on Sunday, August 9, 1981. Almost 40 years later, neither the plane nor its occupants have ever been found, making it Australia's biggest single unsolved civil aviation incident since World War 2.

Finally, a mystery disappearance that is more geographical, than having been caused by man.

Lake George

Just 40km north of Canberra, lies Lake George, an ephemeral body of water that has inspired artists, boating enthusiasts, and historians since the 1800s. Lake George has become one Australia's mythical mystery's due to its disappearing water.

In 1820, Lake George was described by Governor Macquarie (who named the lake after the king) as "a splendid sheet of water". But by 1839 it was dry enough to drive a team of camels across the middle. When the water returned to the lake it then became a resort, complete with paddle steamers plying the waters carrying tourists on scenic cruises.

In 1850 a local grazier stocked the lake with Murray cod and by 1870 there were so many fish in the lake that a trawler worked the lake, netting the fish commercially. Unfortunately, soon after the trawler arrived, the lake did one of its famous disappearing acts and the fish subsequently died due to lack of water.

By 1907 local observers were left reflecting on the "neglected boathouses, jetties and decaying boats" which lay rotting on its once attractive shoreline. Myths and legends surrounding the lake have circulated almost as frequently as the changing water levels. The most colourful legend surrounding Lake George was that a Loch Ness-type monster was occasionally reported lurking in the murky depths. That is when it was full of water. An official warning was issued in 1866 by the NSW Road Guide "to be careful of a large water monster that occasionally surfaces for air".

Since 1949, 13 people have died in the lake's seemingly placid waters, including most famously five naval cadets from Duntroon who drowned when their boat overturned in freezing water in 1956. That only added to the many myths surrounding the lake which have all largely been dismissed.

To many people it still remains "an eerie place" that "has built up an enviable reputation for ghosts, hauntings, UFOs and strange phenomena".

While experts believe the water is regulated more by precipitation from the heavens rather anything mystical beneath, the mystery of its missing water has led to it becoming one of the most studied lakes in Australia.

Sources: *Australian Geographic*, National Museum Canberra, Excerpts from *The Newsman* (Brolga).

Subterranean Secrets

Digging first drains

In 1981 I became privy to one of Melbourne's many hidden tunnels secretly earmarked for an emergency evacuation of the Queen and British PM Margaret Thatcher during the Commonwealth Heads of Government Meeting (CHOGM). In December, 1988 I then witnessed two urban explorers as they set out to explore other secret tunnels, unaware of creatures that almost cost them their lives.

Secrets Under the Surface

Just as arteries and veins ebb and flow beneath the surface of the human body, so too does a similar system sustain the heart of a city. An underground mesh of pipes delivers life-sustaining water through one network, while a series of drains expel our human waste through another. If ever this system fails, then the effects can be terminal for both, as it very nearly was for the city of Melbourne in the 1800s. Had it not been for a system of tunnels and drains that began construction in 1870, Melbourne would have undoubtedly drowned in the slime of human excrement or died from multiple diseases that flowed down city gutters, such as typhoid, diphtheria, tuberculosis, measles and scarlet fever.

Today the old drains still exist. Hidden rivers continue to flow and while new tunnels are being dug, old ones are being rediscovered. The drains still pose dangers but only to the brave and foolish who risk their lives and the laws to crawl and wade their way through this underground labyrinth, tracing a course back through these 'portals into our past'.

In December 1988, I stood on the banks of Melbourne's Yarra River to watch two modern day urban explorers set out on a journey 'back to the future' — back to the source of what was termed the "dismal swamp" by historian Natasha Szuhan. What made this swamp so dismal in the 1800s was the human excrement and animal waste continually being dumped into this cesspool of fermenting filth. Initially it was a natural swamp fed by a tributary or creek named 'Hawk's Burn' which ran from the nearby Malvern Hills, just east of Melbourne. But when it rained the fetid wash, with its familiar stench, began to overflow and the 'Dismal Swamp' also became known as 'Valley of Death' and 'Slough of Despond'. Down it flowed, churning and spewing its detritus through the cheap low-floored worker's cottages in Prahran and on into the Yarra — until the underground drain was built.

On Anzac Day, 1986, a little-known group called the 'Cave Clan' was formed by three teenagers with a bent for crawling through and exploring Melbourne's old forgotten drains. Two members approached me on the condition of anonymity to explore the possibility of a TV news story. Two young men in their late teens who were prepared to risk a stiff $20,000 fine, which was the penalty for being caught in this forbidden subterranean world. We agreed there would be no cameras on this occasion. This would be a 'dry run' to plan logistics. We arranged to rendezvous at an entry point not far from the Prahran railway station, near a culvert that ran alongside a local sporting field. This was the original source of that 'Dismal Swamp' and one of Melbourne's original drains.

The so called 'Maze Drain', may not be Melbourne's largest interconnected system of drains and maintenance tunnels, but according to my intrepid explorers it was the hardest and most confusing to navigate. Hence the dry run. So, I watched as they climbed down the steep bank and began wading along the shallow waters of the Yarra towards a dark black hole ahead of them. I felt they were more concerned about breaching their own code of secrecy by contacting us, than being caught by the law. There was a final furtive check around to see if anyone was looking. My response was the same but by the time I turned back, they had disappeared. And that would be the last time I ever saw them.

From their previous experiences and a copy of their rudimentary map, I was able to trace their journey into the dark, dank and dangerous drain: down metal ladders, through rusty grates, passed rank and reeking waterfalls — and on towards our meeting place. I was aware their first sensory reaction on entering the wide red bricked passage would be its musty smell, and the sound; almost silent, except for a scurrying rat, an occasional cricket or cockroach and the dripping water which trickled down a central culvert.

The trickle blended into a dull rumble from constant traffic passing overhead. And as their light faded they would switch on the beams of their torches, highlighting the walls covered in graffiti. As they had warned, there were many unknown extensions ahead of them, which led off beneath the city and the suburban grid. Some tunnels were dry while others carried remnants of original streams which still flowed occasionally. The end to some extensions were marked on their map as 'manhole covers' opening onto a suburban street or local football field, to be used as possible escapes in the event of a quick exit. Not likely on this trip as the bureau had forecast fine warm weather. The rule of their unwritten law was 'Rain, then no drain'. Ahead of them the drain extended roughly 5km with many offshoots and junctions along the way.

The first chamber was described as large and familiar as it represented a regular meeting place of the Cave Clan members, similar to the nearby 'Anzac Drain' so named because the clan discovered it on Anzac Day in 1986 and used it primarily for initiation ceremonies for new members. After passing through the Maze Drain they planned to continue towards a pair of massive steel pipes, where twin streams of water converged into an underground inlet of the river. Then they would proceed to a corrugated tunnel which snaked towards a glimmer of light from the outside world.

Another entry on their map featured a nondescript culvert which descended into another drain system (G.O.D Drain). This came with a warning of "a deep descent through a gaping metal mouth and a slippery wet stairway washed by a dirty stream of water cascading down a drop of roughly seven to eight metres". To reach the next section they planned to climb a warped metal ladder propped against one side of the waterfall. Its rungs were twisted, its limbs buckled, but the top end was held in place by an old chain attached to the tunnel wall.

Their descriptions have largely matched those of other similar minded urban explorers who have also written of their experiences. Resting at the top they had planned to use their time to catch their breath and snack on their prepacked Mars Bars. However, given my knowledge of the disease and filth that once flowed before them, eating or drinking anything in that environment would have been my last choice.

The break was needed for the next stage called 'The Shrinker' where the wide tunnel narrowed into a square passage. It then became smaller forcing them down on their haunches. This is where they had been warned that claustrophobia usually strikes. Other clan members likened their experiences to "crawling on knees, sucking up fresh air like an addict before detox". The air was now putrid with just the occasional relief from passing drains.

Several hours after leaving them on the banks of the Yarra I estimated they would be approaching the final leg of their 5km trek which would lead to our planned meeting place. My instructions were marked as a secluded culvert at the end of a long, shallow gully which ran the length of an enclosed area beside a grassy playing field, not far from the original site of 'The Dismal Swamp'.

But they never arrived. By late afternoon, as I was preparing to notify my concerns to police, I received a call from The Alfred hospital. They were safe but the horror of their final leg would leave a profound effect on their lives.

Shocked, bloodied and bruised they emerged from another outlet some distance from our planned meeting place. Their injuries would heal, but the mental impact from the creatures they had encountered would take some time for them to recover. As they later wrote: "We hadn't travelled far before we began to notice cobwebs. At first they caught in our hair as we brushed through them." As they continued to crawl through the dry, dusty pipes they began swinging their hands in the darkness in a bid to clear a path through the hanging webs. The further they crawled the thicker the webs became and for the first time they even thought of turning back. Knowing the batteries on their torches were running low in power they were forced to switch them on at brief intervals and in those almost subliminal moments they noticed movement on the walls around them. One fading torch beam finally highlighted a spider. Panic then broke out in that cramped space as dozens more began spiralling down their webs directly in their path. "They were only small but there was no disguising what they were, by their round black bodies with bright red stripes down their backs."

That's when the pain began. A deep throbbing pain in hands and legs. They both knew they had been bitten and both knew, while not necessarily fatal, there were no guarantees. Now frantically waving their arms and shouting they struggled forward on bleeding hands and knees. For some reason they wrote "we screamed and shouted in an effort to frighten the buggers away".

Thankfully the tunnel opened up a little and, as they brushed and ducked to avoid further trailing webs, they rushed through the passage until a glimmer of natural light directed them into a passing drain and out into open air. From there they hailed a cab straight to The Alfred hospital. They did recover from their ordeal but vowed never to return again and I never pursued it. The failed TV story did however give an incredible insight into the Cave Clan members, some of whom would later corroborate similar experiences. But unlike my two urban explorers, none were prepared to break clan rules and invite media into their secret domain. So, as we say in television news, 'no pictures, no story'.

What started as three Melbourne teenagers sneaking into drains soon became the largest consolidated group of urban explorers with chapters in all capital cities around Australia. Perhaps they do it for altruistic purposes but their story has become more of a tribute to the engineering skills of those who built our underground systems to save the greater systems above. While 'Macca' and 'Rocky' renounced any further plans to explore subterranean Melbourne, others took their place. And as Melbourne boasts one of the largest tunnel systems in the world, said to extend over 1500km, there is much to be discovered.

Author's note: My thanks to 'Macca' and 'Rocky' and their fellow urban explorers. To Daron Richter a freelance writer and photographer, and to other members of the 'Cave Clan' who wish to retain their anonymity.

Melbourne's Tunnels

Long before the Cave Clan culture emerged in 1986, the myths and legends of Melbourne's hidden tunnels were never far from the surface. Confirmation of their existence was always difficult to verify as many were dug without official planning permits, built privately or by the military under the Official Secrets Act. Therefore, we were left to depend on a system of 'Chinese whispers' — stories passed on by squatters, adventurers or those who claimed actual knowledge. But like the tunnels themselves these stories are now buried along with part of our history.

Queen's Escape Tunnel

In 1981 I first became aware of Melbourne's hidden tunnels following details of another well-kept secret. Police and anti-terror experts had drawn up plans to utilise the intricate web of underground tunnels for the protection of visiting heads of state, including Her Majesty the Queen and British Prime Minister Margaret Thatcher.

Melbourne was about to play host to CHOGM and security officials were nervously planning for any terror-related contingencies. Three years earlier on February 13, 1978 a bomb had exploded outside Sydney's Hilton Hotel during the first ever CHOGM, marking the first major terrorist incident in Australia. The bomb, which had been planted in a rubbish bin, exploded when the bin was being emptied into a garbage truck in the early hours of that morning. The explosion instantly killed two garbage collectors. A police officer who was on duty at the hotel died later in hospital from his injuries while eleven other people were injured by the blast.

In 1981 every effort was being made to avert a repeat of that incident during CHOGM. Part of the city's security included the installation of thousands of closed-circuit TV cameras. Despite the prying electronic eyes, creating widespread protests against threats to civil liberties and social privacy, the security teams continued to step up surveillance and evacuation procedures.

But security measures for CHOGM were not confined to the controversial eyes around and above the city. The largely secret labyrinth of tunnels beneath the city was also being considered as possible evacuation routes in the event of a major threat to any of the many international leaders and visiting heads of the state, including the Queen and the British PM. One such tunnel beneath Melbourne's Prince Henry's hospital in St Kilda Road Boulevard had been given top priority. Former HSV7 colleague and police reporter Pamela Graham was granted special access to the tunnel by senior sergeant Bill Kelly, a leading anti-terror expert who went on to become Deputy Commissioner in Victoria.

The tunnel was considered because of its position, linking Prince Henry's to the Police hospital on Melbourne's St Kilda Road Boulevard. The former Victoria Police hospital operated as a hospital for some 65 years from 1914 and was not only the first police hospital in Victoria, but was claimed to be the first in the world. During World War 1 it was used as a military hospital and then for the public during the Spanish influenza outbreak, with the police resuming control of the site in 1920. It was from this site an elaborate tunnel had been constructed linking to Prince Henry's hospital and the nearby Yarra Riverbank where boats could continue with evacuations.

It's believed other tunnels which still exist in the same area were also investigated as possible evacuation routes but details were not released for classified reasons. While CHOGM was a complete success and free of any major incidents, the tunnel remained one of the many backups to security and remained until the demolition of Prince Henry's in 1994. There was a certain irony in the demolition of Prince Henry's as it made way for an even larger tunnel — The Metro Rail Project.

Victoria Barracks

VicRoads confirmed during construction of the Metro Rail Project that it had encountered a number of tunnels running from the Victoria Barracks under St Kilda Road, but refused to elaborate. It has long been reported that there was a boat moored near Swanston Street on the Yarra River during World War 2, and in the event of an air raid, the occupants of the War Room near the city would be rushed up the river to the safety of a bunker system near Dights Falls. There are reports that a large underground 'bunker' at Abbotsford was large enough to hold several thousand people.

Hospital Tunnels

Prince Henry's was not the only hospital tunnel to play its part in Melbourne's underground history. In 2011 the Royal Melbourne hospital provided a weekend of public access to its secret tunnels during which over 1200 visitors experienced the elaborate system linking it to the Royal Women's, the Royal Children's, Melbourne University and the former dental hospital in Grattan Street. Between 1942 and 1944 the tunnels became part of the US Army's 4th General hospital with enough space to treat up to 35,000 wounded and sick from the Pacific War.

CBD Tunnels

It's estimated Melbourne's maze of caverns, drains and bunkers stretch 1,500km from the city to the outer suburbs. It has long been reported they run beneath every major street, with the main tunnel system described as being constructed of "beautiful red brick and bluestone rocks designed for horse and carts to transport goods from the docks and big enough to cater for today's trucks". Some are said to have street signs, indicating the corresponding street above.

A number of Melbourne's tourism operators have confirmed their existence but are unable to include them on their specialised tours, for health and safety reasons. The tunnels are said to have linked almost every major city landmark including St Paul's Cathedral, the Regent and Princess Theatres, Parliament House, the Supreme Court and the Old Melbourne Gaol.

Gold Vaults

The underground gold vaults in the Old Treasury Building, are a legacy of Victoria's Gold Rush, commissioned in

1857 to store the gold bullion pouring into Melbourne. An underground railway was pulled by horses connected to government buildings on Spring Street and the Treasury Gold Vault.

Parliament House

Original tunnels under Melbourne's Parliament House have endured since the 1850s, although today they have been adapted for ventilation, plumbing and cabling. While these tunnels have been accessed during special open days, urban legends suggest another set of tunnels were connected from Parliament House to nearby houses of ill repute, allowing certain MPs to access prostitutes without the scrutiny of the press.

SEC Tunnel

One of the largest and most fiercely guarded of Melbourne's tunnels ran directly under the Central Business District (CBD) from the former State Electricity Commission building in William Street. As one former employee recalled, "It was about 90 metres long and more than wide enough for a car to drive through".

Myer Tunnels

A union dispute on a city construction site between Myer and David Jones in September 2012 revealed several tunnels linking the two department stores. They came to light amid allegations that scab labour avoided union picket lines by entering the site through these tunnels. As one unionist claimed, "I'm not sure why they were trying to hide how they got into the site, as numerous underground tunnels were out in plain sight of everyone".

Merri Creek Tunnel

Acting on a tip off from a local resident, solicitor-turned-historian Mark Rawson believes he found the entrance to a secret network of military tunnels near the Merri Creek, Northcote. Despite many years of digging he remains convinced he will one day discover a cache of weapons, unexploded ordnance or toxic chemicals left behind by the Americans who permanently sealed the tunnel at the end of the World War 2.

Melbourne Boy's High

There have been many stories of tunnels under the Melbourne Boy's High School to provide General Douglas Macarthur with a potential escape route from his headquarters at the school during World War 2. The school strongly denies he was stationed there, however there is significant evidence of a tunnel linking the school to the nearby Anzac Drain, which may have been used as a munitions store.

Squizzy Taylor

In November 2013 workers unearthed a tunnel hidden under the streets of Richmond, believed to have been used by legendary Melbourne gangster, 'Squizzy' Taylor, to elude police during raids on his Goodwood Street gambling den during the 1920s. It all adds to the many 'Myths and Mysteries' of a tunnel system and a Melbourne 'underworld' that was not always associated with crime.

Tunnels to Nowhere?

Deep beneath most Australian cities there exists a labyrinth of secret tunnels, drains and decommissioned rail lines buried and largely forgotten. Many have been sealed, bypassed or never documented as part of city planning in the first place. From Townsville to Tasmania and from Perth to Picton, these secret portals are now opening up to reveal our hidden past.

Subterranean Sydney

Sydney not only boasts a splendid harbour with two of the world's most iconic landmarks, but beneath the city lies a fascinating history among its forgotten foundations. Unlike most other cities, alongside Sydney's hidden drains lies a labyrinth of forgotten train lines. In fact, it has been reported there are as many disused or decommissioned railway tunnels under Sydney as there are ones in use.

But not all tunnels beneath the harbour city were built for trains. This has occurred because of the massive growth of the city since the first railway tunnel was cut in 1855. It has now been revealed that there are at least three tunnels lying under Sydney Harbour. The first, sunk near Birchgrove Public School in Balmain, became Sydney's only coal mine. It was dug between 1897 and 1902 to mine coal almost one kilometre below the harbour floor. The second tunnel under

Sydney Harbour, which preceded the current road tunnel by 70 years, passes under Sydney Harbour from Long Nose Point on the tip of the Balmain Peninsula to Greenwich many hundreds of metres above the original coal mine tunnels in the same vicinity.

In February 2020 a hidden tunnel, part of Australia's wartime history, was uncovered by road maintenance workers at Waterfall in Royal National Park. It is believed around 40 other tunnels could be in the Illawarra region alone. Many of Sydney's hidden tunnels have never been documented and those who spoke of their existence years ago have now long passed. It has been left to a new breed of young urban explorers to plot their existence, which they say are large enough in parts to drive a vehicle directly beneath the city streets above.

Families of former employees at Grace Brothers and David Jones, remember tunnels used by delivery vehicles to allow ease of access and the transfer of goods between their stores. Some tunnels were said to have been used as command posts by the Prime Minister and his Cabinet during World War 2. Rumour has it that a series of four tunnels were dug by convicts in the 1820s linking Old Government House to another location in the central Parramatta district. Rumours are now being proven and stories given credibility as cities around the world have discovered their own subterranean past.

Adelaide

Adelaide, which boasts beautiful architecture above ground, has another equally fascinating history buried beneath. Historians and local enthusiasts have devoted years to investigating intricate underground labyrinths and top-secret tunnels. While some remain unconfirmed, new subterranean spaces have been discovered.

The Treasury Tunnels, which date back to 1839, are without a doubt the city's most inviting. Originally built to link key government buildings around Victoria Square, the tunnels and connecting basements were also used to store everything from important state documents to printing materials during the mid 1800s and early 1900s. The Treasury Vaults are the most famous of these storage spaces, having housed nearly 13 tonnes of gold between February 1852 and February 1853 alone.

The nearby King William Street Tunnel is far less inviting — currently filled in with rubble — but adds another layer of history to the city's underground network. Rediscovered in 1973 but deemed too expensive to restore, the tunnel was initially built as a way to transport livestock across the busy road without obstructing traffic. A number of air raid shelters were built around the city during World War 2, further adding to its subterranean landscape.

Perth

Likewise, in West Australia, tunnels built during World War 2 to support one of Rottnest Island's nine-inch guns have been popular with tourists for many years. But just a few hundred metres away are tunnels that are not open to the public — and are probably the most significant of the island's underground network. They contained the 'plotting room', where strategies for protecting Fremantle were considered and assessed in the face of a Japanese threat in World War 2. A tunnel network exists under the Fremantle prison, including a one-kilometre connection to South Beach in South Fremantle. It was built by prisoners, but the purpose was not to enable escapes; their labour was used to provide the prison, and later the town of Fremantle, with a supply of fresh water. The shafts and tunnels have now been restored and opened to the public. However, of all cities in Australia it is Melbourne which boasts the largest labyrinth of tunnels in the world extending over more than 1500km.

Mystery of Buried Bullions

It is estimated that should all buried treasure around Australia be recovered it would be sufficient to wipe out the national debt, even after the economics of the coronavirus pandemic. From pirates to bushrangers, stories of buried booty have long been the source of rumours and myth. But as intriguing treasure tales continue to emerge it adds another element to the list of unsolved mysteries.

The Kimberley Diamonds

The mystery of the Kimberly diamonds is an extraordinary story involving a wartime escape, violent deaths and a secret package involving an estimated $20 million in diamonds that were lost, found, then lost again.

It began on the night of March 3, 1942. Japanese forces had swept down through Indonesia and were about to take one of the last allied airstrips at Bandung, Java. As a camouflaged KLM DC-3 was about to take off with terrified Dutch refugees on board, the manager of the airport ran across the tarmac with a package. He crawled on board through the main hatch, staggered up the sloping central aisle and presented the package to the pilot with urgent instructions to deliver it to the Commonwealth Bank head office in Sydney, Australia. According to eyewitness accounts there was no paperwork involved, just a package the size of a cigar box, covered in brown paper and stamped with the wax seals of the Bank of Java. He then left the aircraft to face his fate with the advancing Japanese.

The pilot, a Russian air ace Captain Ivan 'Turc' Smirnoff then taxied to the end of the strip and took off, bound for Broome. However, on reaching the Kimberley coast the ill-fated DC-3 flew straight into the path of three Japanese Zeros returning from a devastating bombing raid on Broome. Under heavy fire, Smirnoff miraculously landed his badly damaged plane on an isolated beach, and with one of his engines on fire steered it into the sea. In the chaos and confusion, the secret package was momentarily forgotten.

Several passengers were killed in the encounter and with Smirnoff badly injured he was forced to send someone back to the wreckage in a bid to retrieve the mystery package. As it was being recovered a huge wave struck the volunteer sending the package into the sea. No-one in the crew was aware of the contents of the package: hundreds of diamonds, worth nearly $30 million in today's value.

Evidence would later corroborate that the diamonds belonged to a Jewish firm based in Amsterdam which had been sent to Bandung, Indonesia to prevent them being plundered by the Nazis. A local Aboriginal person who witnessed the attack on the DC-3, while walking from Broome to a mission at nearby Beagle Bay, raised the alarm and a search party was organised. The survivors and the injured pilot were finally rescued after spending six days on the beach.

It was only as Smirnov was later being questioned during treatment in a Perth hospital that authorities discovered the contents of the mystery package. Meanwhile, a beachcomber known as Jack Palmer had sailed his lugger to Carnot Bay to check out the wreckage of the downed DC-3. Palmer's stories about what happened would vary over the next 12 months. He first claimed to have found the package washed up on the beach and the diamonds simply fell out.

Palmer then sailed north to Pender Bay and shared some of the smaller diamonds with two friends and exchanged others for sexual favours before going to authorities with some of the larger diamonds inside a salt-shaker. But these represented only a fraction of what was in the original package. Small quantities of diamonds then began turning up around Broome and in the nearby Aboriginal community of Beagle Bay.

In March 1943, a tailor from Broome, Chin Loong Dep, was arrested with 460 diamonds in his possession. He pleaded guilty to receiving them from an unknown Aboriginal boy. Palmer was subsequently arrested but later acquitted, sticking to his story that he had handed over all he found to authorities. After the war Palmer never really had to work again. He bought a house in Broome, a blue Chevrolet, a boat and his business always seemed to be well cashed up. Palmer died in 1958. The epitaph on his headstone in the Broome cemetery simply reads 'Diamond Jack Palmer'. Smirnov returned to flying for KLM, married an American heiress and retired to Majorca where he died in 1959.

Today the wreck site at Carnot Bay has been renamed 'Smirnov Beach' where visitors can still be seen sifting through the sand. In the end the Dutch authorities only recovered seven per cent of the missing diamonds.

But not all our missing treasures are believed buried around our rugged coasts.

Sources: Broome Historical Society, State Library of Victoria, Ozatwar. com and Juliet Wills.

Bushrangers Buried Booty

Frederick Ward

Otherwise known as 'Captain Thunderbolt', Frederick Ward is regarded as the longest roaming bushranger in Australian history and as such made many rich hauls across much of northern New South Wales during his infamous career. But on May 25, 1870, after robbing travellers near the Big Rock, Ward was shot and killed by Constable Alexander Binney Walker at Kentucky Creek near Uralla. As for the proceeds from his career, it apparently went with him to the grave. Many believe it to be buried somewhere around the parts he frequented, and while they have searched, its hiding place still remains a mystery.

There are those who also believe Ned Kelly stashed his stolen booty around Glenrowan and the Strathbogie Ranges in Victoria. Others dispute that theory as nonsense, on the grounds that the Kelly gang were renowned big spenders and "couldn't hold on to anything except a horse's rein."

Ben Hall

Ben Hall was regarded as being a better bushranger than Ned Kelly and had it not been for Ned's dramatic 'last stand' New South Wales locals believe Hall's escapades would be far better known. In the most daring of an estimated 610 robberies, Hall and seven of his gang held up a coach laden with bullion from the goldfields outside Eugowra in 1862. This was reported as the greatest robbery in Australian history. But on the morning of May 5, 1865 he was ambushed and shot dead by the police with little more just £74 in his pockets. Many believe he buried his bullion in the Weddin Mountains outside Grenfell but as he was killed in his final shootout the secret also went with him to the grave.

Frank Gardiner

Once referred to as the 'Father of Bushranging', Frank Gardiner was a man shrouded in mystery. He went by several names, such as Francis Christie and Francis Clarke. Where he was born is uncertain. And no-one really knows what happened to all his share of the takings from that large gold robbery near Eugowra, NSW in 1862. Frank was part of the Ben Hall gang and legend has it that Gardiner had relatives living near Queanbeyan, where he stayed in hiding after the Eugowra robbery. While some of the Eugowra gold was recovered in Forbes, mystery still surrounds what happened to Gardiner's share.

Heathcote Burial

Another bushranger's booty is said to be buried near Heathcote in central Victoria. This gold was the proceeds from a hold-up in which four members of a gold escort were shot. Years afterwards, it was reported a group of mystery men appeared at the spot where the hold-up had taken place, claiming that they had information the gold was buried nearby. It was significant in as much as one of the men had journeyed from Canada saying he had been given information by a friend who had escaped after taking part in the robbery. He claimed the gold had been buried in the hollow of a nearby tree. The three other bushrangers were caught and hanged. The land is now private property, and although several attempts have been made to locate the buried treasure, nobody has been successful.

Maitland Treasure

Four thousand sovereigns were believed buried in a number of bottles by an old gold miner during the bank crisis in the 1890s in a field at West Maitland, New South Wales. Some eight years later, while ploughing a paddock, a young farmhand picked up a pickle bottle full of sovereigns. It's believed the recovered sovereigns were among those buried by the old gold miner who died shortly after hiding his fortune only to be buried himself near the same spot where the bottle was found. The other bottles were never recovered.

As historian's have written, one day some lucky wayfarer will kick aside an old tree stump, dig up a sod of dirt, discover a hidden cave or rummage through a pile rubbish and come upon some buried treasure. However, it may not be the bullion of pirates or the booty of bushrangers. There were others who also buried their wealth.

Inverloch Treasures

Inverloch, a seaside holiday resort and fishing port east of Melbourne, attracts hundreds of visitors each year. But the area also draws a band of treasure hunters seeking millions of dollars said to be buried beneath its shifting sands. Tales first emerged back in 1877 with the theft of a large shipment of freshly minted gold sovereigns from a passing ship on route from Sydney to Sri Lanka. Prime suspect was the ships carpenter Martin Wiberg (also spelled Weiberg or Wyberg) who eventually returned to his coastal home near Inverloch. Police eventually tracked him down and brokered a deal with Wiberg, who took them to a location where they recovered up to 1800 gold sovereigns in a sunken kettle.

No more of the gold was found until 1904, long after his death, when a farmer near Inverloch found a stash of 75 similar gold sovereigns while chopping an old tree for firewood. In all, 1775 were recovered, meaning 3225 solid gold sovereigns with a minimum present-day value of about $2 million are still missing.

In an interesting twist, local historian Annie O'Riley discovered Wiberg's property was eventually sold to local pastroralist, Peter Clemment, adding another mystery to the same property that centred around the disappeance of Margaret Clemment, the so called 'Lady of the Swamp'.

Then in 1925 another local, Mr James Price, said to have been a direct descendent from a family of original white settlers in the Inverloch area, died from a sudden stroke. It seems James didn't trust the banks and had told his family he had buried his life savings of 160 gold sovereigns and jewellery but failed to reveal its location before he died. Word soon spread triggering another treasure hunt in the area. It was never found.

James Price was not alone in his distrust of banks. In the late 1890s a Melbourne-based shipping company operated by local man John Nicholson had amassed great wealth by smuggling food into famine-struck China during the first Sino-Japanese war (1894–95). Nicholson and syndicate members did not trust the banks and decided to bury their combined fortune, worth £200 million on Nicholson's Inverloch property. When his partners died, John Nicholson was left in charge of the treasure. He confided to his grandson, Donald, that the gold would be locked in a steel vault and buried in nearby Savage's Hill, but insisted the money not be touched until Donald was 21 years of age. According to Donald Nicholson, he quarrelled with his grandfather when he was 20, one year short of his agreement, and was told, "You can search for it yourself, even if you have to dig up the whole of Savage's Hill".

And he did, spending most of his life sinking shafts and digging tunnels in his search for the £200 million. So confident was he in locating the missing money he even bought himself a new Mercedes Benz car.

In 1940 he finally wrote to Governor General Lord Gowrie asking for help in his search. The army was called in at the direction of the Chief of the General Staff and a twelve-member team, including four experienced mining engineers, conducted investigations for a week and then prepared to blow up the face of the cliff. At the last moment, an order came from army headquarters directing the search to be called off. No reason was given for the change of plans.

As the years passed, Donald Nicholson now aged in his 70s, became more intense and withdrawn. Locals referred to him as 'The Hermit' from Inverloch. In September of 1954 it was reported that Donald hired a group of specialists using a radioscope (an early version of a metal detector) finding evidence of a large metal object less than 20 feet from the surface.

A short time later, on October 5, 1954, it was reported that Donald Nicholson had taken ill and was rushed to a Melbourne hospital where he died from a stroke. Right up until the end Donald still believed that the treasure was just days from being found. When the object was finally dug up, it proved to be nothing more than a long narrow deposit of black coal. Over the following years Donald's wife Lillian and two of her sisters continued their search, confident the treasure would be found. It hasn't, but the myth is still very much alive.

Source: Annie O'Riley www.oddhistory.com.au

Lasseter's Reef

Then there is the quintessential Australian story of buried gold. Just before the turn of the 20th century, 17-year-old Harold Lasseter set out on foot from Alice Springs to the West Australia goldfields to make his fortune. Somewhere along the way he claims to have found his fortune. Then he lost it. The problem was he couldn't remember where he found it. Thus began the legend of 'Lasseter's Reef', a supposed 14-mile long, gold-rich quartz-ironstone outcrop somewhere west of Alice Springs. Since then, many have wandered into the desert with visions of discovering Lasseter's Reef. Lasseter died in 1931 while on just such a search. Others were destined to follow, wasting countless hours and spending small fortunes in search of the greater find.

Lasseter's Reef became legendary when the largest inland expedition since Burke and Wills was launched, but like Burke and Wills, the expedition was doomed when dissent broke out among the ranks. Facing bankruptcy, the South Australian government funded Lasseter's last expedition, not because they thought he was right, but in the hope that subsequent gold fever would encourage many of the city's unemployed to leave Adelaide. More than 110 years later, not one ounce has been found. The reef remains buried but the legend lives on.

Pirate Benito's hidden treasure

Thursday January 8, 1990 was what we describe in the media-industry as a quiet news day, or the silly season. I had no assignment until 10:00am when I received a phone call stating, "I found the site of Pirate Benito's hidden treasure at Queenscliff. Are you interested?"

A quick call to the State Library of Victoria, and a returned fax containing background details on Pirate Benito and I agreed to meet. Until then I was unaware that local historians had long investigated the exploits of a pirate called 'Benito Bonito' and were equally ignorant of tales of hidden treasure along the southern Victorian coast around the town of Queenscliff.

According to my new information, Benito plundered

under a pseudonym to protect his real identity as Captain Bennett Grahame, a former British naval officer, who had turned rogue. The crew of his vessel were given the option to join him or be put ashore in Panama. Those who opted to leave were subsequently executed — thus he became known as 'Benito Bonito of the Bloody Sword'.

His career as a pirate can be traced back to 1818 when Benito sailed the Spanish Main plundering gold and jewels from the churches and treasury of Lima, Peru. In one of his most infamous exploits he is said to have discovered plans that Spanish gold was being transported by uniformed guard from the Mexican cordillera to Acapulco. He simply captured the guards, put their uniforms on his crew and loaded the treasure onto his own ship. Not a shot was said to have been fired. According to one of many legends, he was pursued by a British man-of-war until separated by wild storms.

Benito is said to have sought shelter as far south as Australia's Port Phillip Bay where he decided to bury his loot in a system of caves near Swan Bay. He then blew up the entrances to conceal his buried treasure with plans to return when it was safe. When leaving the safety of Port Phillip Bay, he suddenly encountered the British man-of-war. Benito and his crew were overpowered and taken to England where they were tried, convicted and duly hanged. A number of his crew were transported to the penal settlements in Tasmania to serve life sentences.

However, one young crew member, a boy named John Karismo, managed to escape. Legends suggest the boy who became known as 'Stingaree Jack' had tattooed the location of the buried treasure on his arm. It's believed he then confided with other convicts who eventually located the treasure and moved part of it to another hiding place at Queenscliff.

On Sunday June 14, 1933 a holiday-maker reportedly discovered an 18th century silver coin near local cliff caves at Queenscliff. The discovery once again revived the legend of Benito's buried treasure. Local Councillor L. J. Romey, who saw the silver coin, confirmed it had been found on the shore of Swan Bay, near the cliffs. "On one side, it had the faint outline of a rose and lion, and experts thought it had been minted in the reign of Queen Anne...".

The Melbourne *Herald* reported the find with the headline: 'The ghost of swashbuckling pirate Benito Bonito is on the march again'. This prompted the local council to allow treasure seekers to dig pits and shafts near the caves, where hundreds had unsuccessfully dug before. The town clerk of Queenscliff, Mr Jack Smith, said at the time that the council had received several requests from syndicates and individuals to be allowed to search for the treasure, which he granted.

In the late 1930s one group financed the most expensive and exhaustive search, headed by a mining engineer who sank timbered shafts and installed boring equipment, pumping equipment and powerful lights in search of subterranean caves. Labourers and divers were also hired, but like all previous attempts their reward was nil.

In January 1990, I met my source in the gravel car park overlooking the township of Queenscliff, south of Geelong. My doubts were raised the moment he stepped from his car holding a metal coathanger, declaring it was his divining rod and would, with great accuracy, pinpoint the exact location of Benito's hidden sword. He led us to the far side of the car park where the gravel made way for the sand dunes and began striding out with his hand-held prong pointing directly ahead of him.

I was preparing to pack up and head back to town when he suddenly yelled, "It's here!" His wire was now pointing down towards the gravel and shaking violently. He had already scraped the shape of a cross excitedly shouting, "it's the same shape as Benito's missing sword". It was only when I stepped further to the edge of the car park I noticed the metal drain pipe protruding from under the car park as an extension to the mark of the cross. His diviner appeared to have worked alright, but Benito's jewel encrusted sword was nothing more than a forgotten drainage system. "No, it's different. Different direction and different depth," he pleaded.

Had I known that the body of Richard III, the last of the Plantagenet dynasty and the last English king to die in battle in 1485, would be found under a council car park in Leicester, central England, I may have stayed a little longer. While the story will no doubt resurface again, one wonders if Benito's buried bullion will.

As Walt Disney once said, "There is more treasure in books than in all the pirate's loot."

Sources: *Herald, The Lure of Pirate Treasure*, Alan Hassell (Trove)

Supernatural Resurgence

Port Arthur

There are those who believe that Australia's dark past of penal settlements and harsh brutality produced a legacy that is now coming back to haunt us. So, it's perhaps not surprising that with so many spirits in our midst, a new age of entrepreneurs is cashing in on a supernatural resurgence.

Monte Cristo Homestead

In 1963, as the new owners turned their car into the driveway of their recently acquired home in the New South Wales town of Junee they noticed lights burning in every room. Just as they were questioning how the lights could possibly operate when power hadn't yet been connected, the lights mysteriously went out. When Reg and Olive Ryan finally moved into their Monte Cristo homestead they soon discovered their lives would never be the same again. The two-storey Victorian manor, built by pioneer Christopher William Crawley in 1885, possessed a tragic history as retold by many of its previous occupants.

The bloodied body of a maid who plummeted to her death off the balcony was often seen at the place she fell, while a young stable boy who was burnt alive could still be heard moaning in the coach house. The ghosts of the original owners apparently refused to leave. The caretaker, who was murdered there in 1961, and a mentally disabled boy who was kept hidden in the homestead's cottage for many years could both be heard crying. A man with mental disabilities, named Harold and who had been chained to a bed for many years, was said to be heard rattling his chains. And the cries of a baby, who a maid claimed was pulled from her arms by an invisible force and thrown to her death down the stairs, were also said to be heard.

Despite visions in the night, including a young woman dressed in white who whispered to Olive, "Don't worry, it will be all right", the Ryan's still decided to stay. Olive says she once found mutilated cats in the kitchen. Visiting children inexplicably threw tantrums around the staircase, where the child had been thrown. There were phantom footsteps, strange apparitions and haunting noises.

In 2014 when Reg passed away, his ashes were spread around the property and like all those who lived and died at Monte Cristo before him, according to Olive, his spirit will also continue to live there. The Ryans not only stayed for 50 years and raised five children at Monte Cristo but capitalised by starting tours of their haunted house.

Studley Park House

On October 15, 1909, the lifeless body of a 14-year-old student at Camden Grammar School (Studley Park House, New South Wales) was discovered in the school dam. Fellow students and teachers carried the body of Ray Blackstone back to the house and kept the body in the cellar awaiting certification for burial.

In 1939, the son of the then owner Arthur Gregory died from appendicitis and as in the case of young Ray Blackstone, the boy's body lay in wait at the house until his funeral. From that moment on there have been reports of visions of two young boys seen playing together. It is also said that the presence of children can be felt throughout the house, while in the tower above stands a lonely woman said to be waiting for the return of her son…or perhaps the next wave of visitors.

Princess Theatre Ghost

In 1990, Melbourne's Princess Theatre reopened after extensive refurbishment by its new owner David Marriner who left just one seat vacant on that opening night for its resident ghost, Frederick Federici. Frederick Baker was a British actor who had migrated to Melbourne and played many roles in Gilbert and Sullivan operas with the JC Williamson company. It wasn't until he changed his name to Federici that his popularity soared.

Then in 1888 in the final scene of the opening of Gounod's opera *Faust*, tragedy struck. Federici, as Satan, was to spirit Faust down to hell. Standing over the stage trapdoor in a mirage of smoke and fire, Federici wrapped his scarlet cloak around his victim. He spoke his character's final lines: "It might be". They were the final lines he would ever deliver before suffering a fatal heart attack as he descended through the trapdoor in the stage.

Ever since then, legend holds that his ghost still haunts the Princess Theatre. A legend upheld by the likes of Bert Newton, Marina Prior and Lisa McCune who claim to have encountered his spirit many times over the years. True or otherwise, management maintained the tradition of saving him a seat for every opening night performance — just in case.

Ghost of Jack the Ripper

There is another Frederick whose name has been recorded among the myths and legends of Australian folklore.

Frederick Bailey Deeming is believed to have been the notorious London serial killer 'Jack the Ripper'. The theory goes that Fred fled Britain in July, 1891 after slaughtering his wife and children and leaving them buried under the floorboards of his home.

Upon his arrival in Australia, Frederick claimed his next victim: a Melbourne woman from Windsor who he disposed of in similar fashion before disappearing into the Australian outback. As Melbourne struggled to comprehend the savageness of the Windsor murder, similarities of the case began to raise international interest at Scotland Yard. While Deeming's movements at many stages of his life are a little obscure, evidence began linking him to England in late 1888, the time of the infamous Whitechapel murders. Frederick was eventually caught by Australian police and duly hanged. When a death mask of Deeming was taken and sent to London it's believed the masks matched the identity of the man police suspected of being Jack the Ripper. The brutality of Deeming's crimes, the timeframe of his movements and the methods of disposing of his victims have led many to believe that he and Jack the Ripper were one and the same.

Melbourne Ghosts

No city boasts its ghosts more than Melbourne, with its haunted houses and narrow laneways. Just down the road from the Princess Theatre, where Melbourne's favourite ghost Federici lives, is the grand Windsor Hotel. It was here Dame Nellie Melba was a regular patron; she met her lovers there and would pay staff for their silence. The ghost of a young teenage boy is often seen guarding Nellie's room where some claim to have heard opera, believed to be Nellie in the throes of passion. Lantern Ghost Tours of Melbourne feature chilling tales of phantom presences who refuse to let the inconvenience of death diminish the enjoyment of their beloved, yet haunted, city.

The Guyra Ghost

The case of the 'Guyra Ghost' or a 'Poltergeist' as it was described in the press, began in April 1921 with "tremendous thumpings" on the walls followed by showers of stones which eventually broke every window in the tiny weatherboard cottage on the outskirts of Guyra, not far from Armidale in New South Wales. Nobody could see who or what was creating the mayhem, but it was soon noticed that the attacks appeared to be focused on 12-year-old Minnie Bowen who lived with her family. Stones smashed through her bedroom window and fell on her bed. Apparently one of the Bowen children confessed to tossing some rocks on the roof to scare the younger sibling, but this didn't account for the extent of the damage that even continued despite a large presence of police at the time of the phenomenon.

Fisher's Ghost

On June 17, 1826, farmer Frederick Fisher left his Campbelltown home in New South Wales and was never seen again — alive that is. His friend and neighbour George Warrell claimed Fred had told him he was leaving for England with no intention of returning. As such George said Fred had bequeathed his home and property to him. Four months after Fisher's disappearance, a man named John Farley ran into the local pub in a very agitated state. He told the astonished patrons that he had just seen the ghost of Fred Fisher sitting on the rail of a nearby bridge. Farley related that the ghost had not spoken, but had merely pointed to a paddock beyond the creek.
Initially Farley's tale was dismissed, but the circumstances

surrounding Fisher's disappearance eventually aroused sufficient suspicion. During a police search of the paddock to which the ghost had pointed, the remains of the murdered Fisher were discovered buried by the side of a creek. George Worrall was arrested for the crime, confessed, and was subsequently hanged.

Many people still report seeing old Fred from time to time. Fisher's Ghost is also remembered in the name of the watercourse, Fishers Ghost Creek which flows through Koshigaya Park, which was created on the site of the paddock where Fred's body was found.

Haunted Picton Tunnel

An abandoned railway tunnel near the New South Wales town of Picton is said to have a resident ghost by the name of Emily. It is believed that Emily was struck and killed while taking a short cut through the tunnel many years ago.

The Redbank Range Tunnel was opened in February 1867, to accommodate the first train service by the New South Wales railways. It was eventually closed in 1919 when a new deviation line opened. During World War 2 it was one of a number of disused railway tunnels used to store ammunition and other military supplies, and more recently the tunnel, now on private property, is used to grow mushrooms. And on any given time, night or day, there are those who will swear they have seen the lonely figure of Emily. And with so many hidden tunnels beneath our cities, Emily may not be alone.

National Film and Sound Archive

In Canberra the grand art deco building of the National Film and Sound Archive preserves more than just historical moving images. Until 1984, it operated as the Australian

Institute of Anatomy, where particular body parts were kept for scientific research. The downstairs corridor, which once housed hundreds of human skulls, is said to be a hive of poltergeist activity, verified by one of the building's contractors who claimed he was pinned against a wall in the basement by a frightening inexplicable force.

Boggo Road Gaol

Queensland's notorious Boggo Road Gaol became one the country's most infamous institutions, known for its harsh punishment and brutal wardens. It also maintained its reputation as a place of execution until 1913 including the only woman hanged in Queensland, Ellen Thomson. Given its long history of rooftop riots, executions and fatal overcrowding, Boggo Road may no longer house dangerous inmates but if tales are true their rebellious spirits still rattle the bars for those prepared to visit the historic site.

Fremantle Prison

An unforgettable experience awaits those prepared to visit the historic Fremantle Prison which "echoes the sounds of loneliness, pain and suffering; of executions gone wrong, where the innocents were unjustly imprisoned and the guilty severely punished". Down among historic tunnels, unexplainable sounds of the many convicts who dug them can be heard, or so the brochure boasts.

We know that in the 1850 shafts were sunk into the limestone bedrock by convicts to provide fresh water from an aquifer offering water to the town of Fremantle. The tunnels were closed in 1910 but have since reopened for tourists prepared to descend deep beneath the former prison.

Above the tunnels, visitors have reported seeing resident ghosts Martha Rendell in the Catholic Chapel and Jack the librarian brushing up on his favourite books. The guide describes them as just two of the poltergeists that roam the cells of this World Heritage listed convict site, which once contained Western Australia's most violent and disturbed criminals between 1855 and 1991.

Fremantle Arts Centre

Not far from the prison stands the Fremantle Arts Centre, formerly an asylum for the criminally insane and reputed to be the most actively haunted building in the state. Doors open and close, faces are seen at windows, strange cold areas are felt, while some visitors claimed to have captured mysterious lights and unexplained images on their cameras. Reported sounds of laughter and crying and a stench of burning flesh from an area once used for electric shock treatment has only added to its frightening reputation as a hotbed of horror that housed the states most troubled souls. And should you visit the centre and have red hair, don't be surprised if you attract the lady who was committed in the 1800s after losing her daughter then losing her mind. Her missing daughter, believed to have been abducted, had red hair and just occasionally a redheaded visitor reports feeling the sensation of having their hair being tugged.

Ararat Mental Institution

The former Ararat Lunatic Asylum in Victoria claims as many as 13,000 patients died within its walls during its 140 years of operation, so the potential for ghost stories is not surprising. Victoria's earliest psychiatric institution opened its doors back in the 1860s, and these days the abandoned building hosts a range of ghost tours around its austere and haunting grounds.

Visitors have reported feelings of being "shoved and bitten" as well as sounds of shrieking voices, ticking clocks and strange images on cameras and other electrical interference.

One particularly infamous room can leave visitors with feelings of "nausea, terror and trance like states" which are said to last until they've left the building. Where are you Elvis?

Port Arthur

Port Arthur in Tasmania, otherwise known as 'hell on earth' by its convict prisoners, was considered one of the worst prisons in the British Empire. The site of Australia's worst mass shooting, added to its tragic past in both modern and post-colonial history.

The village and historic site, built in 1830, served as a convict settlement for hardened criminals —many of whom succumbed to its brutal conditions. Many of their spirits are said to still roam the grounds.

Some claim to hear the sounds of ghostly children crying in the solitary 'separate prison' and see disembodied faces appearing in the dissection room under the surgeon's house. But one of the main focal points is the parsonage where a restless figure of its former vicar is said to reside. In the last two decades, around 2000 paranormal incidents have been recorded. The museum even has an 'unusual occurrence form' on hand for anyone wanting to report their own unworldly incident.

Sources: State Tourist Offices and Libraries of Melbourne, Adelaide, Sydney and Perth

****

Joss paper, also known as ghost or spirit money, are sheets of paper made into burnt offerings. The procedure is common in Chinese ancestral worship to ensure the spirit of the deceased is adequately cared for in the afterlife. Today 'ghost money' takes on a new meaning as tourists continue to be drawn to haunted houses in the hope of experiencing a taste of the afterlife. But be warned, there are just as many haunted homes not on the tourist map.

Myths or Legends

Hanging Rock

A *legend* can be an unverified story handed down by tradition associated with historical events or people, past or present, who inspire legendary fame. A *myth* is traditionally an ancient story dealing with supernatural beings, unique ancestors or heroes of the past. What is fact or fiction is for you to decide.

Myths, Legends or Folklore

Australian mythology is steeped in a history dating back to the beginning of time. From our First Nations' Dreaming during which cultural and spiritual stories were born came 'Rainbow Serpent', 'Wagyl', 'Tiddalik', 'Muldjewangk', 'Devil Pool', 'and 'Black Mountain'. Then there are the legends and folklore that have emerged since settlement, to be dismissed or accepted depending on how the story has been told and what you are prepared to believe.

Hanging Rock

The story begins on Valentine's Day in 1900 when a group of four schoolgirls and their headmistress from the elite Appleyard College, arrived at Hanging Rock for a picnic. Believed drawn to the rock's mystical formation they enter one of the many crevices and passageways to make their way up to the misty summit. That was the last time they were seen. Only a hysterical and confused student by the name of Edith made it down, however she was so traumatised and dazed by her experience that she lost all memory of what happened.

The story originated from a novel by 71-year-old Joan Lindsay who gave ambiguous answers when asked whether the story was based on fact or fiction only suggesting it was a mix of both. However, Peter Weir's hauntingly popular film only strengthened the legend of the rock's mysterious past.

Less commonly known as Mount Diogenes, the volcanic rock rises dramatically from a plain 70km northwest of Melbourne. Stories passed down by the rocks original indigenous owners have indicated the importance, both culturally and spiritually, that it played in their lives. Legend has it that the site was inhabited by evil spirits and used for sacred and initiation ceremonies.

Nevertheless, more recent events have also added to the mystique of Hanging Rock and these stories have largely been verified by media and police documents. On New Year's Day 1901, a young family arrived for a picnic, just as the schoolgirls did in Joan Lindsay's story. Leaving his wife at the base, 37-year-old James Flight planned to climb to the summit with his two children but, halfway up, he told them to go back down because the going was too difficult. That was the last time they would see him alive. Witnesses told police they saw him reach the summit before plunging to his death 60 feet below.

To compound the mystery the *Bendigo Independent* on January 17, 1901, carried the headline: 'Murder or Accident at the Hanging Rock?' Nobody could explain how he met his gruesome end and the coroner was eventually forced to concede that his death had been accidental. A year later, a six-year-old boy named 'McRae' was found wandering at Hanging Rock in a dazed condition; his face covered in blood. He was apparently too traumatised to explain to an attending doctor, or police, what caused his injuries.

In 1907, there was a murder at the rock but this time the assailant, a 19-year-old man, was caught by the police and duly sentenced. And so, the legend of Hanging Rock grew.

Novelist Joan Lindsey admitted she wrote her story in less than four weeks, raising questions at the time that she may have been channelled by some unseen force. Odd occurrences and coincidences were a feature of the late Joan Lindsay's life who often referred to clocks strangely stopping in her presence. Those odd occurrences apparently also occurred during filming of the Peter Weir production. Prior to the launch of the film I reconnected with its co-producer Patricia Lovell who I had first met a few years earlier while she and Bruce Webster were co-hosting the early morning *Today* show in Sydney (ATN7). I was briefly hosting the Melbourne version on HSV7.

It was then she revealed how 'slightly bemused' she had been during the shoot by so many watches belonging to the film crew regularly stopping for no apparent reason. "All our watches played up during filming that it became quite a joke."

When an audience finally gathered at Melbourne's State Theatre in 1975 for the Victorian premiere of the film, the theatre clock mysteriously stopped. Today Hanging Rock continues to attract the tourists, luring them in by its mythical charm just as it did on that fateful day as told in the story of *Picnic at Hanging Rock*.

The Hawkesbury River Monster

It has been described as Australia's own 'Nessie", and like its namesake this mythical creature raises its head from time to time from the depths of the Hawkesbury River, north of Sydney. Or so we have been told.

After researching the so called 'river monster' since 1965, cryptozoologist Rex Gilroy claimed he too had seen the 12m giant break the surface of the Hawkesbury back in 2009. In supporting his claims, he cited indigenous Australians who he says recorded this creature long before colonial times. Remote Hawkesbury Aboriginal rock and cave paintings are said to illustrate a creature similar to a plesiosaur, an extinct marine reptile which is known to have existed during the Jurassic Period.

Among reports over the years, one published in the *Windsor and Richmond Gazette* in 1924 generated widespread interest when observers described it as a 'titanic seahorse'. More recent eyewitness accounts describe the 'Moolyewonk' as having a long neck, flippers and a distinctive grey colour. Mr Gilroy supports the theory that the creature is a plesiosaur from the Jurassic period but doesn't believe it's the only one in local waters. "There are areas of ocean," he said, "where anything could live down there and you wouldn't know."

Burning Man Mystery

A Victorian cleaner from the town of Warrnambool has become known as 'The Burning Man'. Frank Clewer had unknowingly built up a 40,000 volt charge of static electricity in his clothes, leaving a trail of scorched carpet and molten plastic as he walked.

The baffling 'Burning Man's' brush with fire was documented in September 2005 when firefighters responded to a call for help. Wearing a woollen shirt and a synthetic nylon jacket,

Clewer had generated a life-threatening voltage of static electricity in his clothing. When he walked into a building in the Victorian town of Warrnambool the electrical charge ignited the carpet. Within five minutes, the carpet had erupted, forcing startled employees to ring firefighters who evacuated the building.

According to one of the firefighters, "We tested his clothes with a static electricity field meter which measured a current of 40,000 volts, one step shy of spontaneous combustion. I've been firefighting for over 35 years and never come across anything like this."

Clewer survived the mysterious 'inner fire' without the slightest lesion on his skin — the only visible evidence being a charred hole in the knee of his jeans. However, after leaving the building apparently unscathed he discovered a burning piece of plastic on the floor of his car, so returned to seek further help from the firefighters. It may have been a one-off event but Spontaneous Human Combustion (SHC) has been inexplicably occurring for more than 2000 years, with one of the earliest recorded events dated 52 BC.

Marree Man

No one knows who carved the drawing of the 'Marree Man' first witnessed by a tour guide in 1998, in the Australian desert. The drawing stretched over 4km and depicted a clear image of an indigenous man. Tourism spiked as word of its existence spread, but this angered some local Australians who wished the drawing would simply disappear. Strangely enough, that is exactly what happened. A news article in 2015 featured photographs showing an almost-blank terrain where the Marree Man had once appeared and just as mysteriously disappeared.

The Dreaming — Traditional Myths and Legends

The Rainbow Serpent

This is the quintessential Dreaming story, and easily the most widely known around Australia. The Rainbow Serpent or Snake is portrayed as a long mythical creature made of different parts of animals such as a kangaroo's head, crocodile's tail with a huge snake-like body. There are countless variations passed down through time depending on which Indigenous culture or language you listen to, but the common theme is that a huge snake slumbered beneath the earth's surface until it emerged to awaken the world and forged the hills, lakes, valleys and rivers from a previously featureless land. One of those formations has the dubious distinction of becoming the most haunted location in Australia.

Devil's Pool

In the middle of a lush Queensland rainforest lies an unsuspecting swimming hole. Known as 'Devil's Pool' it has long been a popular destination for Australian hikers and backpackers travelling up to Cairns. However, behind its innocent serenity and clear inviting waters it possesses a mythical power that has drawn many to their deaths.

The legend begins with a young woman named Oolana who married an elder from her own tribe. Yet shortly after they married she fell in love with another man named Dyga from a rival tribe. The two lovers ran away from their tribes and fled to what is now known as Devil's Pool where they were captured by the elders. Oolana broke free and leapt into the water while calling for Dyga to follow her before she drowned. According to legend her cries for her lost lover can still be heard and has been luring men into the pool ever since. Devil's Pool has claimed 17 lives since 1959 and was eventually fenced off with the epitaph, "He came for a visit …and stayed forever".

Black Mountain

Black Mountain in Far North Queensland near Cooktown is also known as 'Kalkajaka' or 'place of spear.' It is a mass of black granite boulders in tropical north Queensland that includes four spiritual indigenous sites where the Eastern Kuku Yalanji Aboriginal people gathered to pass down their many Dreaming stories.

Aboriginal Dreaming stories also describe the mountain as a haunted place, home to various evil spirits and demons lurking within. The historical stories of Black Mountain assumed extra significance after European colonisation, when colonists, their horses and mobs of cattle would regularly disappear into gaping crevasses between the boulders never to be seen again. The first of these dates back to 1877, when a man went out towards Black Mountain on horseback, looking for a stray calf. Widespread searches were conducted but neither the calf, the horse or the man returned and no trace of them was ever found.

Many have fallen victim of the mystery of Black Mountain. Two police officers entered the mountain while investigating a missing case. Only one officer made it out alive but was so traumatised that he was later determined to be insane. Two cavers and trackers who also entered the mountain, disappeared, while a backpacker named Harry Page appears to have been the only person whose body has ever been recovered although the cause of his death was unknown.

Beneath the outer boulders lies a maze of passages and chambers blamed for enticing explorers, the inquisitive or those seeking to hide from pursuers. In the ink dark interior, sheer drops, pockets of bad air or unexpected encounters with snakes or bats are believed to cause panic and injury to those who dared enter. In addition, pilots have reported aircraft turbulence and magnetic effects above the mountain while loud, strange noises and mournful cries have been heard from others who have camped on ground close to Black Mountain.

Geologist Gavin Dear who lived near the foot of the mountain doesn't believe in the myths, which he described as ridiculous. He believes the disappearances are due to mishap rather than mystery but concedes the mountain does possess a mystifying special power. Enough it would seem for Black Mountain to be dubbed the 'Bermuda Triangle' of Queensland.

Muldjewangk

Deep in the Murray River of South Australia lurks a terrible race of creatures known as the 'Muldjewangk'. Details of the creature vary. Some say that they are a race of merfolk. Others describe it as a giant monster. But one thing is constant: they are not particularly friendly. Supposedly hiding under clumps of floating seaweed, the Muldjewangk destroy fishing nets and disturb those who are foolish enough to enter their territory. Though some local elders claim that the Muldjewangk no longer exist, but they still tell their stories to keep their children from playing by the river after dark. Today we call them Bunyips.

Tiddalik

The 'Tiddalik' is a character in Aboriginal Dreamings. While not the creator like the Rainbow Serpent, it still plays an important role in Aboriginal spiritual beliefs. Although tales of the Tiddalik are widespread, they actually are all derived from the First Nations people of South Gippsland, Victoria. The Tiddalik is a giant water-holding frog that once drank all of the world's fresh water. When everything began to die of thirst, the other creatures devised a plan to make Tiddalik laugh, thereby releasing all of the water in his mouth.

Many creatures tried to make him laugh, but all failed until 'Nabunum' the eel danced and twisted himself into knots before him. Laughing, Tiddalik released the water, refilling the world's lakes, swamps, and rivers. While this restored water to the world, it also had the adverse effect of causing a massive environmental flood drowning many of the creatures or stranding them on different islands.

In modern times, the story has evolved into children's books with a far happier ending.

Wagyl

While the Rainbow Serpent created the universe and humans, the 'Wagyl' was assigned with creating and protecting rivers, lakes, springs, and wildlife. Much like the Dirawong, the Wagyl is believed to have a physical body which slithered over the land, carving out the paths of rivers. Whenever he stopped to rest, his body created bays and lakes. His scraped-off scales became forests and woodlands while his droppings became piles of rocks. Strongly associated with rivers, the Wagyl is said to be personally responsible for the creation of the Swan and Canning Rivers and the other waterways around Perth and south-west West Australia. The Noongar people believe that they were assigned by the Wagyl as the guardians of their land.

Yara-ma-yha-who

This creature measures around 1.2m tall with bright red skin and is regarded as one of the most fascinating creatures in legendary Australia. The 'Yara-ma-yha-who' (think Drop Bear) is a carnivorous creature that lives in the trees and feeds on those unfortunate enough to pass below them. It possesses one of the strangest methods of consuming its prey in all of Aboriginal creation stories. Once it locates its prey, it jumps down on top of them and sucks out most of its blood. It uses octopus-like suckers on the ends if its fingers and toes to hold on while it feeds. After the victim is sufficiently weakened from blood loss, but still alive, the Yara-ma-yha-who will swallow them whole. After falling asleep, the Yara-ma-yha-who will then regurgitate its victim. Upon waking, they will swallow the victim again. The process of eat-and-regurgitate will continue over and over again until the victim, who is usually alive throughout the entire process, becomes a new Yara-ma-yha-who.
Sleep well.

Sources: Britannica, National Library of Australia, www.aboriginal-art-australia.com

****

Just as we began by acknowledging the mythical monsters and billabong beasts, let me end by acknowledging the original custodians of this great land, to thank the many contributors for their stories and the State Libraries of Victoria and New South Wales who provided vital access to our unexplained history.
As I have explained there is always a risk to credibility and a price to be paid by becoming too subjective in journalism.

Objectivity was taught as the benchmark by which stories should not be influenced by personal feelings or opinions when reporting facts. I may not pursue the beliefs portrayed in every story in this book but I have to the best of my ability recounted the Myths, Mysteries and Legends as recorded by their original contributors.

Even a memoir primarily focuses on fact.

ORDER

Aussie Myths, Mysteries and Memories
Mal Walden

ISBN: 9780648697039		Qty
RRP	AU$24.99	.....
Postage within Australia	AU$5.00	.....
	TOTAL* $_____	
	* All prices include GST	

Name: ....

Address: ....

....

Phone: ....

Email: ....

Payment: [ ] Money Order   [ ] Cheque   [ ] MasterCard   [ ] Visa

Cardholder's Name:...

Credit Card Number: ....

Signature:..

Expiry Date: ....

Allow 7 days for delivery.

Payment to: Marzocco Consultancy (ABN 14 067 257 390)
                     PO Box 452
                     Torquay Victoria 3228
                     Australia

Be Published

Publish through a successful publisher.
Brolga Publishing is represented through:
• National book trade distribution, including sales, marketing & distribution through Simon & Schuster.
• International book trade distribution to:
 - The United Kingdom
 - Sales representation in South East Asia
• Worldwide e-Book distribution

For details and enquiries, contact:
Brolga Publishing Pty Ltd
ABN 46 063 962 443
PO Box 452
Torquay Victoria 3228
Australia

markzocchi@brolgapublishing.com.au
(Email for a catalogue request)